HIGHLAND DANCING

Dedicated to

Jack Muir
Chairman of the Scottish Official Board of Highland
Dancing until his death in December 1967,
whose technical skill and devotion to Highland Dancing
made this book possible

Highland Dancing

The official textbook of
The Scottish Official Board
of Highland Dancing

NELSON

THOMAS NELSON AND SONS LTD
36 Park Street London W1
P.O. Box 2187 Accra
P.O. Box 336 Apapa Lagos
P.O. Box 25012 Nairobi
P.O. Box 21149 Dar es Salaam
77 Coffee Street San Fernando Trinidad

THOMAS NELSON (AUSTRALIA) LTD
597 Little Collins Street Melbourne C1

THOMAS NELSON AND SONS (SOUTH AFRICA) (PROPRIETARY) LTD
51 Commissioner Street Johannesburg

THOMAS NELSON AND SONS (CANADA) LTD
81 Curlew Drive Don Mills Ontario

THOMAS NELSON AND SONS
Copewood and Davis Streets Camden New Jersey 08103

Printed in Great Britain by
Thomas Nelson (Printers) Ltd, London and Edinburgh

Scottish Official Board of Highland Dancing

Office-Bearers

President	Brigadier Alasdair G. L. Maclean, C.B.E., of Pennycross
Vice-President	Doctor Alistair C. McLaren, T.D.
Chairman	
Secretary/Treasurer	Miss Marjory Rowan

Delegates

Dance Associations

British Association of Teachers of Dancing	Miss J. Ritchie	Miss C. G. Stewart
British Ballet Organisation	Miss A. Calder	Miss K. Garland
Highland Dancing Specialists' Association	Miss M. G. Falconer	Miss J. Symington
North British Ballrooms Association	Mrs I. Macdonald	Mr A. Fusco
Royal Scottish Country Dance Society	Captain J. Bain	Mr J. Oliver
Scottish Dance Teachers' Alliance	Miss E. Haggart	Miss C. M. Robertson
United Kingdom Alliance of Teachers of Dancing	Miss C. Tucker	Miss P. MacDonald
Australian Board of Highland Dancing	Miss A. Calder	Miss B. Jessiman
Southern California Highland Dancing Association	Mr W. Forsyth	

Her Majesty's Forces

The Army	Major R. W. Smith

Games Associations

Cowal Highland Gathering	Mr H. Matheson
Thornton Highland Gathering	Mr T. Nicol
Bute Highland Games	Mr T. B. McMillan

Independent Members

Mr J. L. McKenzie, Miss N. M. Ross, Miss J. Stewart, Miss E. P. Wallace, Miss J. H. Lindsay, Mr S. Bell, Miss M. F. Lindsay, Miss E. G. Strathern, Mr W. M. Cuthbertson, Major A. A. Bourne, Brigadier H. J. D. Clark (*Honorary*), Captain T. S. Davidson (*Honorary*), Mr Harry Fairlie (*Honorary*).

Affiliated Members

Australian Board of Highland Dancing, Official Board of Highland Dancing (South Africa), The Piping and Dancing Association of New Zealand, The British Columbia Highland Dancing Association, Caledonian Club of San Francisco, Highland Dancers' Association of Ontario, Southern California Highland Dancing Association, Quebec Highland Dancing Association, Northern California Highland Dancing Association, Eastern Canada Highland Dancers' Alliance, Pacific International Highland Games Association, Alberta Highland Dancing Association.

Rules and Constitution

1. *Title*

The Title of the above Board shall be the 'Scottish Official Board of Highland Dancing' and hereinafter referred to as 'The Board' and its address, 8 Regent Terrace, Edinburgh, or such address as may be appointed from time to time.

2. *Definitions*

(*a*) An Association, Organisation or Society having representation on the Board shall be known as a Represented Member.

(*b*) Any person entitled to sit on the Board as a representative of a Represented Member shall be known as a Delegate.

(*c*) Any person who, although not a delegate, is entitled to sit on the Board by virtue of Rule 8 (para. c), shall be known as an Independent Member.

(*d*) An Association, Organisation or Society outwith Scotland, having representation on the Board, shall be known as an Affiliated Member.

3. *Objects*

Subject to the proviso that it shall in no way interfere with the business and/or administrative arrangements of the Societies and Associations represented upon it, the objects of the Board are:

(*a*) To bring about co-operation between the recognised associations, societies, games organisations and individuals connected with Highland Dancing.

(*b*) To educate the public to take lessons from qualified teachers.

(*c*) To help the public by seeing that all recognised teachers show similar basic steps for the traditional dances.

(*d*) To see that the S.O.B.H.D. Rules are observed in all Championships and recognised Competitions.

(*e*) To encourage the proper conduct of competitions, to recognise certain established championships as such and to discourage the duplication of such events.

(*f*) and generally, to do anything that will advance the art of Highland Dancing and preserve its traditional form.

4. *Technique*

The Board will appoint a Technical Committee consisting of teachers of dancing and other individuals who may or may not be members of the Board but who are recognised authorities on Highland Dancing.

The Board will recommend the dances which could be used in Competitions and Championships.

The Board will define the basic steps and movements which may be used in the above dances.

The Board will determine the technical points which shall guide a judge towards arriving at a decision.

5. *Judging*

The Board will determine how many judges are required and what their qualifications must be to judge (*a*) a Competition, (*b*) a Championship.

6. *Amateurs*

The Board will determine what constitutes an Amateur, what rewards he or she is eligible to receive, and the procedure to be adopted against amateurs who infringe the rules.

7. *Championships*

The Board will grant licences for the organisation of Championships, see that these are properly carried out and take care that titles are not duplicated.

8. *Constitution*

The Board shall consist of:

(*a*) Two representatives from each of certain approved Societies or Associations.

(*b*) One representative each from Highland Games Organisations, approved by the Board.

(*c*) Not more than ten Independent Members, who shall be selected by reason of their knowledge and experience of Highland Dancing.

(*d*) An Honorary President.

(*e*) A Chairman who, previously to election, may or may not be a member of the Board.

(*f*) The Board shall meet four times a year at least, or as required. Ten members will form a quorum.

9. *Office-Bearers*

The Hon. President, Chairman, Secretary and Treasurer of the Board will be known as Office-Bearers. Their duties shall be as follows:

(*a*) *Hon. President:*

The Hon. President may, if present at a Board meeting, open and/or close the meeting if he so desires but otherwise shall not preside. He shall be accorded the same privileges as a Delegate or Independent Member.

(*b*) *Chairman:*

(1) He shall preside at all meetings of the Board, but in his absence, at any meeting, the members shall elect a Chairman for that particular meeting.

(2) He shall inspect and announce the result of all voting.

(3) He may give his casting vote in the case of a tie, but otherwise shall not vote.

(4) Prior to the expiration of his term of office he shall ensure that the Annual Balance Sheet is duly audited and distributed to all Affiliated, Represented and Independent Members.

(*c*) *Secretary:*

(1) He shall record the minutes of all Board meetings which shall be read and confirmed at the next meeting.

(2) He shall notify all Affiliated, Represented and Independent Members of each Board meeting giving at least 14 days' notice.

(3) He shall send a report of the minutes of each Board meeting to all Affiliated, Represented and Independent Members.

(4) He shall have care of all books and papers relating to his office.

(5) He shall pay over to the Treasurer from time to time, or on request, all moneys received by him on behalf of the Board.

(6) Any expenses outwith normal petty cash expenditures he may incur on behalf of the Board may, if it be so decided at a Board meeting, be defrayed out of the funds of the Board.

(*d*) *Treasurer:*

(1) He shall have charge of and be responsible for the funds of the Board, whatever form they may take, and shall pay all accounts passed by the Board.

(2) He shall, when required, render a true account of all the moneys received and paid by him on account of the Board.

(3) He shall, when required, bring to a Board meeting all books and documents relating to his office.

(4) He shall, when required, pay over all funds remaining in his hands and assign and deliver all books, papers and property belonging to the Board, to such person or persons as the Board shall appoint.

(5) He shall prepare and present a Balance Sheet annually or when called upon by the Board to do so.

10. *Appointments*

(*a*) Delegates shall be nominated by the Society or Association which they represent and in the event of a Delegate being unable to be present at any meeting of the Board, the body which he or she represents may nominate a substitute for that meeting, but it shall not be the right of any Independent Member to nominate a substitute.

(*b*) A Society or Association which desires to be represented on the Board shall make application, in writing, to the Secretary of the Board and shall satisfy the Board that:

(1) It is firmly established and has a proper set of rules which are strictly followed (copy of said rules must accompany application).

(2) It only receives as members, those who pass a properly conducted examination of a standard up to that required by the Board.

(*c*) The name of any new nominee for Independent, Represented or Affiliated Membership, or any new applicant for Independent, Represented or Affiliated Membership of the Board shall appear on the Agenda for the Board Meeting at which the matter is to be considered.

11. *Re-election*

The Societies, Associations and Independent Members, will be subject to Annual Re-election at the A.G.M. and for the purpose of such re-election, it shall suffice if the Society, Association or Independent Member is proposed, seconded and secures a majority of the votes of those present.

In the event of one or more Independent Members ceasing to be a member of the Board, for any reason whatsoever, the Board shall have power to elect another person to the vacancy.

12. *Publicity*

It is not permissible for any Member of the Board to advertise the fact of his or her membership in any advertisement, circular or letter heading. It is permissible, however, to obtain wherever possible, editorial reference to the Board and its work in the Press, even if this entails publication in the interview or article of some member's name.

13. *Subscription*

Any Society or Association represented on the Board shall pay an annual subscription, the amount for each year to be fixed by the Board from year to year; this subscription shall become due as soon as the amount has been fixed.

14. *Committees*

The Board shall have powers to appoint committees to deal with specific matters. Such Committees may include non-members of the Board. Each committee must appoint a Convener who must report the work of the committee to the Board. The Chairman of the Board is an ex officio, a member of all committees.

Whilst a committee is functioning, the convener of such committee, if not already a Delegate or Independent Member of the Board shall ex officio be co-opted to the Board and accorded the same privileges as a Delegate or Independent Member.

15. *Emergency Meetings*

It is the duty of the Chairman to call a meeting of the Board, should he be requested to do so, in writing, by not less than ten Delegates and/or Independent Members of the Board. The meeting must be called within two weeks of the date on which this request is received.

16. *Election of Office-Bearers and Committees*

(*a*) Office-Bearers shall be elected by ballot at the A.G.M.

(*b*) Members of all Committees shall be elected by ballot at the Annual General Meeting, but should a new committee be necessary, such committees may be elected, by ballot at a Board Meeting provided that all nominations for such new committee appear on the Agenda for the meeting at which the ballot is to take place.

(*c*) Retiring Office-Bearers and retiring Members of the Committee shall be eligible for re-election, but new nominations for any of these posts must be in the Secretary's hands at least 28 days prior to the A.G.M. and the names of such new nominees shall appear on the Agenda for that Annual General Meeting.

(*d*) Should there be a vacancy in any of these offices or on any Committee, the Board may appoint some person to fill that post until, the next election.

17. *Arrears*

(*a*) An Independent Member whose subscription is 3 months in arrears, or the Delegate or Delegates of any Represented or Affiliated Member whose subscription is 3 months in arrears, shall not be allowed to speak or vote at any meeting of the Board.

(*b*) If still in arrears at the end of 12 months any Independent or Affiliated Member may be struck off the roll of Membership of the Board.

(*c*) The names of all Independent Members and/or Represented and Affiliated Members of the Board whose subscriptions are 3 months in arrears shall be read out at each Board meeting.

18. *Funds, Books, etc.*

(*a*) All moneys subscribed or paid out and all property acquired on behalf of the Board by the Treasurer or the Secretary shall belong to the Board.

(*b*) Any Office-Bearer, Delegate or Independent Member misapplying the funds of the Board shall repay the same or be expelled from the Board and shall be further liable to prosecution for such misapplication.

19. *Auditors and Financial Year*

(*a*) The financial year of the Board shall end on 31 August.

(*b*) Three Delegates and/or Independent Members shall be appointed each year by the Board to audit the accounts of the Board and shall examine the Annual Balance Sheet and Returns. They shall report to the Board the result of the audit.

20. *Board Meetings*

(*a*) The date of the Annual General Meeting shall take place in November of each year, the exact date to be fixed at the Board Meeting at least 3 months prior.

(*b*) The Standing Orders shall be read at the opening of the Annual General Meeting, and if approved, adopted.

(*c*) At the Annual General Meeting and at any Board Meeting at which a ballot is to take place, scrutineers shall be appointed to count the votes and report the results to the Chairman, and fulfil any other duties required.

(*d*) Unless by the permission of the Board or upon the invitation of the Board, no person or persons other than the Office-Bearers, Delegates and Independent Members designated by rule 8, shall be present at a Board Meeting.

21. *Expulsion*

(*a*) Should the conduct, act or acts of any Independent, Represented, or Affiliated Member of the Board be, in the opinion of the Board, an infringement of the Bye-Laws, Rules or Regulations of the Board, directly or indirectly detrimental to the interests, welfare or reputation of the Board or any of its objects, then such Independent Member, or in the case of an Affiliated or Represented Member a deputation, should be requested to attend a meeting of the Board and it shall be in the power of the Board at such meeting or any adjournment thereof to expel the offending Independent, Represented or Affiliated Member from Membership of the Board if so determined by the votes of three-quarters of the combined number of Office-Bearers, Delegates and Independent Members of such meeting, but an Independent, Represented or Affiliated Member so expelled from Membership of the Board shall have the right to appeal at a special meeting of the Board called upon the requisition of at least 5 Delegates, and/or Independent Members of the Board. Any Independent, Represented or Affiliated Members so expelled from Membership of the Board shall forfeit all claims on the funds of the Board.

(*b*) The repetition of private business and/or confidential matters discussed at any Board Meeting to any persons not directly or indirectly connected with the Board will be considered detrimental to the interests and welfare of the Board and will evoke the penalty as in paragraph (*a*) of this rule.

(*c*) Should an Independent Member be frequently absent from Board meetings the resignation of that Independent Member may be requested should it be so decided at a Board Meeting.

22. *Alteration to Bye-Laws*

No alteration to these bye-laws shall come into force until it has received the assent of two-thirds of those voting at a meeting of the Board and has previously been set out in the Agenda for such meeting.

Acknowledgments

Gratitude is due especially to the following members of the Board, who have rendered invaluable service: Miss Jean J. C. McLellan, who was for two years one of the S.D.T.A. Delegates, and who carried out the secretarial duties during the formation of the Board; Captain T. S. Davidson, who succeeded Miss McLellan in the Secretaryship and carried it on until forced, for reasons of health, to resign; and Mr D. G. McLellan, whose co-operation we still happily enjoy.

Valuable services have also been rendered by the following former Delegates and Independent Members: Miss M. Brown, Miss B. Findlay, Colonel A. Gordon, Miss M. F. Hadden, Mrs P. Keay, Miss J. McLellan, Mr D. G. McLennan, Dr A. Robertson, Mr B. Robertson, Major A. D. Rowan Hamilton, Miss A. Stewart, Mr R. Thomson.

Note on Illustrations

The occasional lack of sharpness in the reproduction of plates numbered 39–70 is due to the fact that they are stills taken from a moving colour film. This film, 'Highland Dancing, Basic Positions and Basic Movements', is the official film on Highland Dancing of the S.O.B.H.D.

Contents

Foreword

By Brigadier H. D. Clark

I count it a great privilege to have been asked by the Board to write this Foreword to the new edition of its textbook *Highland Dancing*. I put away my dancing shoes some years ago and I am no longer a practising member of the Board. But I was one of its Founder Members and Judges and, during my years of Army service, I, in a manner of speaking, danced my way round the world. That brought me in contact with many of the Caledonian and St Andrew's Societies in far away places, including Peking, and convinced me that a love for Highland and Scottish Country Dancing is a characteristic of those of Scottish birth and blood who live and work in oversea countries.

Those who introduced Highland Dancing to communities overseas introduced the technique in which they were originally instructed, and there grew up a tradition of dancing in different techniques in the various parts of the Empire, now Commonwealth, and foreign countries. These differences in technique were not confined to the 'exiles' for there were variations in steps and movements at home, and, as is stated in the Introduction to the textbook, competitors at Games were subject to conditions and judgements which varied according to the fashion of a particular district. It is a far cry from the original Highland Dancing competitions of the Highland Society of London at the beginning of the nineteenth century, when such dances as 'A Twasome Strathspey' and stringed music were in vogue. As interest in competition grew with the passing of the years and instruction became authoritative the dancing technique became more defined. Such noted dancers as the MacLennan family set out their technique in book form and the Games in Scotland adopted certain Highland Dances for competition. So too did the Games organisers overseas, and overall there was a reasonable community of ideas on what to dance and how to dance in the Highland fashion. But there were differing ideas on technique and judging.

The Introduction explains how the Official Board came into being and what it set out to do. I was one of those who met in Stirling in January 1950, and I can testify to the devotion of those who took service on the Board at that time and have continued to serve it to this present time. One of those is the Chairman of the Board today, Mr Jack Muir, who has set us all an example of loyalty and faith and has guided us in our approach to a traditional and accepted technique of Competition Dancing. There are also those who have accepted the duty of judging the dancing at Games at home and of instructing in technique and judging overseas. They deserve the support of organisers and competitors everywhere. The influence of the Board has spread to Commonwealth and other countries, as is evidenced by the number of Affiliated Members and their contacts with the Board at home. There is still room for the Board's presence in the administration of some of our Highland Games in Scotland.

One original delegate to the Board whose name I must mention is the late Bailie J. F. Stewart. His work for the Board and in the cause of Dancing, and his organising of the annual International Festival of Dancing in Edinburgh, were of great value to all concerned in the development of dancing technique and dancing talent. He was particularly concerned to bring more young boys and men into the Highland Dancing Competition field and it is hoped that his aim will be fulfilled in the years ahead. Highland Dancing is for men as well as women!

I have many memories of dancing and dancing friends, but I will confine my closing words to a tribute to my colleagues on the Official Board with whom I worked. They were an inspiration to me, just an amateur, and I learned much of technique and friendship in my association with them, and I also gained the firm conviction that the Board is doing an essential service to Highland Dancing and all who love dancing in the Highland fashion.

This revised edition of the Board's textbook is the consummation of dedicated and searching enquiries into and assessment of advice and recommendations for amendment of the original edition from its wide membership, through the Technical Committee. I commend the book as authoritative to all devotees of Highland Dancing.

Introduction

In any particular country the evolution of a national form of dancing is bound to give rise to diverse opinions as to the correct method of performing that country's traditional dances unless it is controlled by some one generally recognised authority. Many of the innovations which have periodically appeared in Highland Dancing were accepted by dancers all over Scotland, but certain brilliant exponents of the art have, from time to time, introduced new ideas and variations of their own. These new ideas were adopted only by the pupils and followers of those who invented them, and there has developed a chaotic situation, in which our traditional dances are danced differently in different parts of our country. Dancers competing at the various games throughout Scotland have had to vary their style and alter their steps according to the district in which they were competing, or according to the known stylistic preferences of the judges before whom they were appearing.

Various associations of teachers, and many individuals well versed in Highland Dancing, have compiled their own descriptions of our traditional dances, and their own versions of the traditional technique. Some of these accounts of Highland Dancing resemble one another fairly closely, but no two of them are exactly alike.

To the organisers of Highland Games, that part of the programme which was concerned with Highland Dancing was a constant thorn in the flesh. Complaints were continually being made to them about bad or biased judging, or about unsatisfactory features in the conduct of the competitions; and there is no doubt that an appreciable percentage of those complaints was justified. Yet the organisers could do little or nothing about them, because there was no generally recognised authority to which they could refer such complaints for consideration and necessary action. Nor was there any body to which competitors having a legitimate grievance against the organisers of, or the judges at, any particular Games could appeal, because the rules laid down by the promoters of any particular competition were not applicable to other competitions, and there were no generally applicable rules governing the conduct of championships or other competitions of lesser importance. Furthermore, there being no rules to give a clear definition of the status of the amateur dancer, the term 'amateur', in most instances, was merely farcical.

Towards the end of the year 1949 the Scottish Dance Teachers' Alliance made a move towards bringing this unsatisfactory state of affairs to an end, by advocating the establishment of a representative board of control. The principal aims and objects of the board would be to stabilise the technique of Highland Dancing, to formulate laws and regulations covering every aspect of the art, and to do everything in its power to further the interests of our national dancing. It was fitting that this first move should have been made by the Alliance, because it is the only association of professional teachers of dancing which can, by reason of its constitution, claim to be purely Scottish. Getting in touch with other associations which foster Highland Dancing, and with various organisations which sponsor Highland Games, the Alliance invited each of these bodies to send delegates to a meeting specially convened for the purpose of considering the advisability of establishing a representative body to control Highland Dancing. Many prominent personalities, well known to the public as exponents (past or present), as judges, or as patrons, of Highland Dancing, but not connected with any professional association, were also invited to attend this meeting. Mr James Adam having kindly offered, for this purpose, the Plaza Ballroom in Stirling, the meeting took place there in January 1950. It was presided over by Mr Jack Muir, who was President of the Alliance at that time, and resulted in the inauguration of 'The Scottish Official Board of Highland Dancing'.

This Board is representative of all organisations and individuals interested in any aspect of Highland Dancing, and its constitution makes provision for: four Office-Bearers; two Delegates each from Represented Members (Scottish Associations or those with Scottish branches) and Affiliated Members (Overseas Associations); one Delegate each from a limited number of Games Organisations; and not more than ten Independent Members.

This book sets forth the stabilised technique of Highland Dancing which has been compiled by the Board and adopted by all associations and individuals connected with that body. This is tantamount to stating that practically every qualified teacher of Highland Dancing in Scotland has adopted that technique. The book also contains rules and regulations, formulated by the Board, pertaining to our national dancing in all its other aspects.[1]

In every part of the world where Scots are to be found, and particularly in every part of the British Commonwealth, there is usually a Scottish Society of some description, and most of these societies are sponsors of Highland Dancing. As ambassadors for this branch of our national culture they look, naturally, to their mother country for guidance. Hitherto they have been in a quandary as to whose description of the Highland dances, and whose version of the technique, they should adopt. Now, with the advent of the Scottish Official Board of Highland Dancing, they have available to them authoritative, practical and comprehensive instructions governing that art in all its aspects.

---

[1] Originally it was intended also to provide a brief but authoritative account of the history of Highland Dancing. Gradually, however, it became clear that the difficulties in the way of such an attempt are at present well-nigh insuperable: reliable evidence concerning origins and early development is scarce and scattered; in the general neglect of Scottish culture which has prevailed, until recently, in all four Scottish universities, Highland Dancing has been largely ignored by learned men; and as yet little or no serious research has been done. There is an opportunity here for academic investigators which, it is to be hoped, they will not fail much longer to exploit.

CHAPTER ONE

Basic Positions and Basic Movements

General Remarks and Preliminary Definitions

1   The body should be held in a natural easy manner without stiffness, strain or exaggeration.

2   The foot supporting the weight of the body is called the SUPPORTING FOOT. The other foot is called the WORKING FOOT. While dancing, it is always the ball of the Supporting Foot that is in contact with the ground.

3   It should be the aim of the dancer to keep the supporting leg turned out at an angle of 45° to the Line of Direction (see p. 3), and the working leg turned out at an angle of not less than 45°—and in many cases 90°—to the Line of Direction. This turning out of the knees tends to keep the apron of the kilt flat.

4   When executing any movement of elevation, the dancer should land on the count except where otherwise stated.

5   When the working foot has to be placed in or raised to any specified position whilst executing a movement of elevation, that foot arrives at the specified position simultaneously with the dancer landing on the supporting foot, unless otherwise stated.

6   (a) BASIC POSITIONS are the essential positions of the feet, arms and head on which all movements are founded.
(b) A BASIC MOVEMENT is the combining, by movement, of two or more Basic Positions.
(c) A BASIC STEP is a combination of Basic Movements.

A. Basic Positions

1. Foot Positions

In this book foot positions are described and illustrated as nearly as possible as they should appear in actual dancing.

Definitions

A CLOSED POSITION is one in which the feet are either in contact with each other, or the working foot is touching the supporting leg. (An exception is Third Crossed Position.)

An OPEN POSITION is one in which the working foot is not in contact with the supporting foot or the supporting leg.

A GROUND POSITION is one in which both feet are in contact with the ground.

An AERIAL POSITION is one in which the working foot is off the ground.

A REAR POSITION is one in which the working foot is to the rear of the supporting foot.

Preliminary Remarks

There are five *basic ground positions* of the feet, namely, First Position, Second Position, Third Position, Fourth Position and Fifth Position. In addition to these there are three *derived positions*: one, being a variation of Third Position is called 'Third Crossed Position'; the other two, both variations of Fourth Position, are called 'Fourth Intermediate Position' and 'Fourth-opposite-Fifth Position'.

In a *ground position* the following terms are used in describing various methods of placing the working foot.

(a) *Toe*. When in contact with the ground, without pressure, in an open position with the instep arched, or in a closed position with the foot vertical, it is said to be *pointed* or placed on the *toe*. When the working foot is pointed in an open position the knee of the working leg is kept straight except when placed in Fourth-opposite-Fifth Position (see page 11).

(b) *Half point*. When the pads of the first two or three toes are in contact with the ground, with the ball of the foot off the ground, it is said to be placed on the *half point*.

When placed on the half point in an open position, the instep of the working foot should be arched with the knee of the working leg slightly relaxed; in a closed position, the working foot should be kept as vertical as possible.

When the working foot is placed on the half point, the weight of the body may be partially taken on it; the main weight being then retained on the other foot, thus providing the impetus for any required slight elevation or travel of that (i.e. the supporting) foot during the half point.

(c) *Ball*. When the pads of the toes and the ball of the foot are in contact with the ground with the instep arched, it is said to be placed on the *ball*, and the knee of the working leg is kept as straight as possible, but *without strain*, to allow for freedom of movement.

When the working foot is placed on the ball, the weight of the body is transferred on to it, so that when the dancer travels while so placing the foot, a step is taken.

(d) *Heel*. When the heel is in contact with the ground, with the sole of the foot kept straight and inclined upwards, the working foot is said to be placed on the *heel*.

The heel is always placed without pressure, except in the Eighth Seann Triubhas Step, in which the weight is momentarily taken on it.

When the working foot is placed on the heel in any open position except Fourth-opposite-Fifth, the knee of the working leg is kept straight.

Certain positions have *rear* and/or *aerial* equivalents. There is no rear or aerial equivalent to First Position or to Third Crossed Position. There is an aerial equivalent, but no rear equivalent to Second Position. Conversely there is a rear equivalent but no aerial equivalent to Fourth-opposite-Fifth Position and to the Fifth Position. Every other position has a rear and an aerial equivalent.

In a *Rear Position*, the working foot is never placed on the half point or the heel.

In an *open aerial position*, the knee of the working leg should be kept straight, and the working foot, with the instep well arched, is off the ground with the toe at the correct height in relation to the supporting leg, to give *normal* level (in line with the centre of the calf), *high* level (in line with the centre of the knee-cap), or *low* level (in line with the ankle).

BASIC POSITIONS

In the two *closed aerial positions*, namely Third Aerial Position and Third Rear Aerial Position, the working foot is off the ground in contact with, and at the correct height in relation to the supporting leg to give *normal* level (foot vertical—heel in line with the hollow below the knee) or, in the case of Third Aerial Position only, *low* level (foot vertical—toe at ankle height) or *very low* level (see note to the description of Shuffle on page 27).

Note.—In all Aerial Positions (Open or Closed), normal level is to be understood where no particular height is specified.

When preparing for and/or landing from a step of elevation with the weight equally distributed on the balls of both feet in Third or Fifth Position, the insteps should be as fully arched as possible, the heels equidistant from the ground, and the knees slightly relaxed.

The Line of Direction

The Line of Direction is an imaginary line on the ground, passing from front to back between the heels of the dancer when standing in First Position. The angles of basic foot positions are measured from this line.

To ensure a correct line of travel when executing steps which travel sideways towards Second Position (e.g. the Second and Eighth Seann Triubhas steps), the working foot should be placed slightly forward or backwards, as the case may be, from Second Position to commence the travel.

First Position

The heels are together, with the weight of the body equally distributed on both feet, which are turned out to form an angle of 90° (each foot being at an angle of 45° from the Line of Direction). The dancer may be standing with both feet flat on the ground (1), or may be poised on the balls of the feet (2).

Second Aerial Position

The working leg is extended to the side as in Second Position, but raised at the required level —low (5), normal (6), or high (7).

BASIC POSITIONS

Second Position

The working leg is extended directly to the side at an angle of 90° from the Line of Direction, the toe and heel of the working foot being in line with the heel of the supporting foot (4). The working foot may be placed on the toe (3), half point, ball, or heel and, except in the latter case, is placed approximately one and a half foot-lengths from the heel of the supporting foot.

Third Position

The working foot, which may be placed on the toe (9), half point, ball (8), or heel, touches the hollow of the supporting foot, each foot facing outwards at an angle of 90° from the other (or 45° from the Line of Direction).

Note.—When the weight is equally distributed on the balls of both feet, the sole of the front foot is directly over the instep of the rear foot.

Third Aerial Position

With the knee of the working leg pressed well back, the outside edge of the working foot is placed in contact with the front of the supporting leg, to give *normal* level with the heel slightly below the level of the knee cap of the supporting leg (10), *low* level with the toe in line with the ankle of the supporting leg or *very low* level with the foot slightly off the ground above Third Position.

Third Rear Position

The hollow of the working foot touches the heel of the supporting foot, each foot facing outwards at an angle of 90° from the other (11, 12). The working foot may be placed on the toe or ball.

Third Rear Aerial Position

The working foot is placed behind the supporting leg at the same height as in Third Aerial Position normal level, the inside edge of the foot being in contact with the calf of the supporting leg (14). The knee of the working leg is held well back, no part of the working foot being visible from the front (13).

Third Crossed Position

The working leg is crossed in front of the supporting leg with the half point of the working foot placed near the outside edge of the instep of the supporting foot (15).

BASIC POSITIONS

Fourth Position

The working leg is extended to the front with both heels in line with the Line of Direction. The working foot, which is placed only on the toe, is turned out at an angle of 45° from the Line of Direction (16).

Fourth Aerial Position

The working leg is extended to the front as in Fourth Position, but raised at the required level (17).

Fourth Rear Position

As in Fourth Position, but the working leg is extended to the rear, and is placed only on the ball (18).

9

Fourth Rear Aerial Position

The working leg is extended to the rear as in Fourth Rear Position, but raised at the required level (19).

Fourth Intermediate Position

The working leg is extended diagonally forward at an angle of 45° from the Line of Direction with the working foot placed on the toe (20), half point or ball.

Fourth Intermediate Aerial Position

The working leg is extended as in Fourth Intermediate Position, but raised at the required level (21).

Fourth Intermediate Rear Position

As in Fourth Intermediate Position, but the working leg is extended to the rear and is placed only on the ball (22).

Fourth Intermediate Rear Aerial Position

As in Fourth Intermediate Rear Position, but with the working leg raised at the required level (23).

BASIC POSITIONS

Fourth-opposite-Fifth Position

The working leg is extended to the front as in Fourth Position, but with the toe of the working foot in line with the heel of the supporting foot and with a slight relaxation of the knee of the working leg. The working foot may be placed on the toe (24), half point or heel and, in the latter case, the heel is placed in line with the toe of the supporting foot.

Note.—This position is used only in the Sword Dance.

25

Fourth-opposite-Fifth Rear Position

This is the position of the rear foot when the front foot is placed in Fourth-opposite-Fifth Position.

Fifth Position

The working foot is in contact with the big toe joint of the supporting foot, and may be placed on the toe (25), half point, ball, or heel, each foot facing outwards at an angle of 90° from the other.

Note.—When the weight of the body is equally distributed on the balls of both feet, the sole of the front foot is directly over the toes of the rear foot.

Fifth Rear Position

This is the position of the rear foot when it is placed on the ball with the big toe joint in contact with the front foot, each foot facing outwards at an angle of 90° from the other.

2. Arm Positions

Grouping of Fingers. In all positions of the arms except First Position, the fingers are lightly grouped and the thumb is in contact with the first joint of the middle finger.

First Position

Both hands rest on the hips with the backs of the hands to the front, the knuckles facing the body with the wrists straight, and the elbows pointing directly out to the side (26).

26

12

BASIC POSITIONS

Note.—When an arm is raised or lowered, there should be a minimum displacement of the elbow, and no part of the arm or hand should come in front of the dancer's face. Exceptions are in the fourth bar of the Introduction to the Seann Triubhas, where the hands come up in front of the face as the arms are raised in front of the body from Fifth Position, and also in the First and Second Seann Triubhas Steps when the arms are circled from First or Fifth Position.

27   28

Second Position

One arm is placed as in First Position, the other is raised at the side, with the arm and wrist slightly curved, the hand slightly above and forward from the head-line, the palm turned inwards (27, 28).

Note.—In this position the raised arm is always on the side opposite to the working leg, except in a Propelled Pivot Turn.

Third Position
Both arms are placed as described for the raised arm in Second Position the palms facing inwards towards each other (29).

Fourth Position
A closer and higher form of Third Position with the hands almost touching (30).

Fifth Position
The arms are gently curved down in front of the body with the hands quite close to each other and the little fingers almost touching the kilt.

14

31

3. *Head Positions*

All head positions are described in relation to the position of the body.

First Position

The head faces the front with the eyes level (31).

Note.—The head is in First Position when the *arms* are in First, Third, Fourth or Fifth Position, except when otherwise stated (31).

Second Position

The head is directed diagonally to the right (32) or left (33), with the chin slightly raised.

Note.—When the *arms* are in Second Position the head is turned away from the raised arm.

32

33

B. Basic Movements

The system on which the counting of movements is based is explained in Chapter Three.

The Bow

Stand with the *feet* and *head* in First Position, *arms* by the side or in First Position. Bow by inclining the body forward slowly, and return to the original position (34, 35, 36).

Note.—The depth of the bow must not be exaggerated, and the timing varies according to each dance, as described in Chapter Two.

34

35

36

BASIC MOVEMENTS

Hop

A movement of elevation begun on the ball of one foot and finished by landing on the ball of the same foot.

Spring

As for Hop, but landing on the ball of the other foot (37, 38, 39).

Step

A transfer of weight from one foot on to the ball of the other foot. Can be executed with or without travel and, where specially designated, the heel may be lowered to finish on the flat foot.

37

38

39

Assemble

A movement of elevation begun on the ball of one foot and finished by landing simultaneously on the balls of both feet in Third or Fifth Position (40, 41, 42).

Disassemble

A movement of elevation begun in a closed position with the weight of the body equally distributed on the balls of both feet, and finished by landing on the ball of one foot with the other placed in, or raised to, a specified position.

Note.—There is no travel on this movement, and, unless otherwise stated, during the elevation there is no extension of the foot upon which the dancer is to land.

40

41

42

BASIC MOVEMENTS

Change

A movement of elevation begun with the weight of the body on the balls of both feet in Fifth Position and finished by landing on the balls of both feet simultaneously in Fifth Position with the other foot in front (43, 44, 45).

Note.—During the elevation there is no extension towards Second Aerial Position. This movement may also be executed using Third Position.

Brush

(*a*) *Outwards:* The working foot lightly touches the ground in its progress from Third Aerial Position Very Low to an Open Aerial Position or from a Rear Position, through First Position to Fourth Aerial Position.

(*b*) *Inwards:* The working foot lightly touches the ground in its progress from an Open Aerial Position to an accepted Closed Position (see Shuffle) or to Third Aerial Position Low (see Hop-Brush-Beat-Beat).

Note.—When an Outward Brush is executed in conjunction with a Spring or a Hop, the working foot touches the ground almost simultaneously on landing.

43

44

45

46

47

Leap

A movement of elevation begun from the balls of both feet in Fifth Position, extending both legs towards Second Aerial Position, and finished by landing simultaneously on the balls of both feet in Fifth Position with or without change of feet (46, 47, 48).

48

Note 1.—On the extension during the elevation, both legs should be straightened.

Note 2.—This movement may also be executed using Third Position.

Shake

A Shake is always executed in conjunction with a Hop.

(*a*) For *Seann Triubhas:* The working foot is progressively extended by two or more subsidiary movements (called shake actions) from Third or Fifth Position to Second Aerial Position High. The shake actions come from the knee controlled by the thigh and they should be started while flexing the knee of the supporting leg in preparation for the Hop, simultaneously on landing from which, the working foot arrives at its highest point.

20

Example for Counting
'and and a 1'.

(*b*) For *Highland Fling:* The movement is always preceded by a placing of the working foot in Third or Fifth Position from where it is extended to Fourth Intermediate Aerial Position using only one subsidiary movement. Thus, the actual Shake movement consists of two shake actions, the first finished with the working foot in Fourth Intermediate Aerial Position Low and the second with that foot arriving at Fourth Intermediate Aerial Position simultaneously on landing from the accompanying Hop.

Examples for Counting
(Including the preceding placing of the working foot.)
'1 and [and] a 2'   or   '1 [and] and a 2'.

49   50

Pas de Basque
Preparing with an extension of the working foot to Second Aerial Position Low (49, 50); spring to that side (51), bringing the new working foot to Third or Fifth Position, placing it on the half point (52); then beat (without exaggeration) the ball of the other foot in Third or Fifth Rear Position, at the same time sharply extending the front foot, if required, to begin the next movement.

Note 1.—The same Position—Third or Fifth—must be used throughout the movement.

Note 2.—When a turn, or part of a turn, is executed using two Pas de Basque, there is no extension to finish the first Pas de Basque, and the second is danced with little or no travel.

Note 3.—This movement may also be danced with other than lateral travel, in which case the extension of the starting foot is along the required line of travel, generally towards Fourth Intermediate Position.

21

Counting

(2 Pas de Basque)

Reel   1 & 2   3 & 4 = (2 bars)

Sword Dance   1& 2 3& 4 = (1 bar)

Open Pas de Basque

As in Pas de Basque, except that the front foot is placed in Fourth-opposite-Fifth Position, and there is no extension at the finish.

Note.—This movement is used only in the Sword Dance, and in the quick steps is also executed using Fourth Position, Fourth Intermediate Position and Second Position.

53

54

High Cut

Spring, hop or disassemble and, simultaneously on landing, take the working foot to Third Rear Aerial Position (53), then (working from the knee joint only) re-extend the working foot towards Second Aerial Position (54) and return it to Third Rear Aerial Position (55). During the elevation one or both legs may be extended towards Second Aerial Position. Unless where specially designated, there is no side travel in this movement.

55

Note.—Performed in series, High Cutting can be described as a succession of Springs from Third Rear Aerial Position to Third Rear Aerial Position, executing a High Cut each time and during each elevation extending both feet towards Second Aerial Position, although this extension of the foot from which each Spring is commenced may be slight.

Counting

(four High Cuts)

(*a*) To Strathspey tempo—1& 2& 3& 4&
In certain stated instances a single High Cut may be counted 1 and [and]

(*b*) To Reel tempo—1 & 2 & 3 & 4 &
In certain stated instances, a single High Cut may be counted 1&   or   1 and [and]

23

High Cut in Front

As for High Cut, but the raised foot is taken to Third Aerial Position (56) and the re-extension is towards Fourth Intermediate Aerial Position.

Note.—High Cuts in Front are not performed in series, and in certain specified cases (e.g. in the Ninth Seann Triubhas Step 'Double High Cutting') the re-extension may be towards Second Aerial Position.

56

Balance

Starting with one foot in Fourth Intermediate Aerial Position and with the shoulder on the same side as that foot slightly advanced, spring on to that foot displacing the supporting foot which is taken to Fourth Intermediate Rear Aerial Position. Repeat *contra* to complete the movement and finish in the starting position. This movement occupies two beats of music. The shoulder on the side of the commencing foot should be slightly advanced.

57

58

BASIC MOVEMENTS

Travelling Balance

Commence with the right foot in Fourth Intermediate Aerial Position, the body facing the front with the right shoulder slightly advanced, the *arms* in Third Position and the *head* in Second Position turned towards the front (57).

Bring the right foot inwards to take three steps RF, LF, RF, travelling diagonally backwards in a line approximately 45° to the Line of Direction, the foot positions being Fifth Position (58), Fourth Intermediate Rear Position (59) and Fifth Position (60), respectively, extending the left foot to Fourth Intermediate Aerial Position (61) simultaneously on taking the third step (Count '1 & 2'). The above is now repeated *contra*, travelling forward along the same diagonal line to finish the movement in the original starting position (57) (Count '3 & 4'). This movement can also be executed on the other side with the opposite foot and is invariably danced to the count '5 & 6, 7 & 8'.

Note.—Throughout the movement, the upper part of the body is held erect.

Arms

The *arms* are taken inwards to Fourth Position during the backward travel then returned to Third Position during the forward travel or, alternatively, during the backward travel they are circled outwards and downwards at the sides to Fifth Position then, during the forward travel, they are circled outwards and upwards at the sides to Third Position.

59

60

61

Rock

Spring from Third or Fifth Position to Third Rear Position, or vice versa, pointing the working foot almost simultaneously on landing. Rocks are usually danced in series, in which case the first Rock may be executed starting from an open position. The rear foot is always pointed first.

Note.—When the working foot is pointed during this movement the toe touches the ground lightly.

Round-the-Leg

The working foot is passed from Third Rear Aerial Position (62) to Third Aerial Position (63) or vice versa. During the movement the working foot must be kept as close as possible to the supporting leg with the knee of the working leg held well back.

Shedding

Hop, spring or disassemble pointing the working foot in Second Position (count '1'); hop, taking the working foot to Third Rear Aerial Position (count '2'); hop, executing a Round-the-Leg movement with the working foot to Third Aerial Position (count '3'); hop, executing a Round-the-Leg movement with the working foot to Third Rear Aerial Position (count '4').

Note.—Second Position of the *arms* is invariably used with this movement, the raised arm being on the side opposite to the working foot.

62

BASIC MOVEMENTS

Toe-and-Heel

Hop or spring and, almost simultaneously on landing, point the working foot in a specified position, then hop and, almost simultaneously on landing, place the heel of the working foot in the same specified position. This movement occupies two beats of music.

Note 1.—The toe and the heel must touch the ground lightly and the working foot must be kept fairly low.

Note 2.—The specified position for this movement may be Second, Third, Fourth-opposite-Fifth or Fifth. The 90° turn out required for the working foot in Second Position should also be aimed for in the other three positions.

Heel-and-Toe

Hop, placing the heel of the working foot in Second Position; hop, pointing the working foot in Third or Fifth Position. This movement occupies two beats of music.

Back-stepping

Starting with one foot in Third Aerial Position, execute a Round-the-Leg movement to Third Rear Aerial Position, and, with a Spring, slide it down the back of the supporting leg, bringing the other foot quickly to Third Aerial Position. Repeat as required. This movement may also be executed starting or finishing in Third Rear Aerial Position. Each Back-step occupies one beat of music.

 63
 64

Shuffle

Starting with one foot midway between Fourth Aerial Position Low and Fourth Intermediate Aerial Position Low, spring or hop and, during the elevation, extend the original supporting foot to midway between Fourth Aerial Position Low and Fourth Intermediate Aerial Position Low, then, almost simultaneously on landing, brush the new working foot inwards to the half point in Third or Fifth Position and immediately brush it outwards to midway between Fourth Aerial Position Low and Fourth Intermediate Aerial Position Low.

27

Note 1.—The Inward Brush is finished without the working foot losing contact with the ground and with the instep slightly relaxed to bring the heel over the instep of the supporting foot, a position referred to as '*over the buckle*'.

Note 2.—Shuffles are executed without lateral or forward travel but, where specified, a slight backward travel may be used.

Note 3.—If the movement preceding a series of Shuffles finishes with the working foot in an Aerial Position other than starting Aerial Position given above, the first Shuffle of the series may be started from there.

Note 4.—When, under certain stated circumstances such as are given in the first note in the Seann Triubhas description, it is necessary to start the first of a series of Shuffles with a Hop instead of a Spring, there is no change of supporting foot during that Shuffle as both the Inward and the Outward Brushes are executed with the starting foot.

Examples for Counting (Four Shuffles)
(*a*) To Strathspey tempo   1& 2& 3& 4&
(*b*) To Reel tempo   1 & 2 & 3 & 4 &

65   66

Spring Point

Spring, and point the working foot in an open position, both feet touching the ground almost simultaneously (65, 66).

Pivot Turn

(*a*) *Turning to the left.* Take the right foot to Third Crossed Position while beginning to pivot to the left on the ball of the left foot (67), and complete the turn on the balls of both feet without displacing them (68), finishing in Third or Fifth Position with the left foot in front.

(*b*) *Turning to the right.* As above, but starting with the left foot and finishing with the right foot in front.

Note.—The working foot may be extended to Fourth Intermediate Aerial Position before starting the Pivot Turn.

BASIC MOVEMENTS

Hop-Brush-Beat-Beat

Hop, extending the working foot to Fourth Intermediate Aerial Position if not already so placed, then quickly execute an Inward Brush to Third Aerial Position Low (count '1 and [and]'); place the working foot on the half point in Third or Fifth Position then lightly beat the rear foot in Third or Fifth Rear Position (count 'a 2').

Note 1.—Simultaneously on executing the beat with the rear foot on the count of '2', the working foot may be extended to Fourth Intermediate Aerial Position or Second Aerial Position according to the starting position required for the movement which is to follow.

Note 2.—The movement can also be executed to the count '5 and [and] a 6'.

Shake-Shake-Down

Hop, executing a shake action with the working foot in Fourth Intermediate Aerial Position; hop, carrying the working foot slightly backwards to execute another shake action with that foot in Second Aerial Position then spring to displace the supporting foot which, if required, may be sharply extended to any aerial position required to start the next movement.

If desired, both shake actions may be executed in Second Aerial Position in which case there is no backward movement of the working foot during the two shake actions.

Note.—The starting position of the working foot depends upon whether or not it has been extended to finish the Hop-Brush-Beat-Beat movement by which it is invariably preceded.

Examples for Counting
'3 & 4'   or   '7 & 8'

Propelled Pivot Turn or Reel Turn

Danced during a Reel by two dancers, facing in opposite directions with the shoulder-lines parallel. The *inner arm* of each dancer is extended diagonally forward and linked with that of the partner, the *outer arm* being in Second Position, and the head turned slightly towards partner.

67

68

69

Note.—'The inner arms linked'—The inner fore-arms rest parallel and are in contact with each other, with the palm of the hand lightly supporting the underside of partner's arm just above the elbow. Since this is not a grip but an aid to balance, the thumb must not encircle partner's upper arm (69).

When danced turning to the right, the movement is begun by the partners moving forward with a slight spring on to the right foot whilst linking their right arms and adopting the position described above (count '1'); they now place the left foot on the half point in Second Position, to allow for a slight travel of the right foot (count '& 2'); the turn is now continued by repeating the actions described for the count of '& 2' as often as required (count '& 3 & 4', etc.) so that, while the right foot takes the main weight of the body, the left foot acts as a propelling force to produce the turn, during which the knees must be slightly relaxed.

When danced turning to the left, the movement is begun by moving forward on to the left foot whilst linking left arms; the left foot then becomes the main supporting foot with the right foot providing the propelling force.

Progressive Strathspey Movement

Beginning with the right foot in Third Aerial Position, step with that foot along the line of travel to Fourth Intermediate Position (count '1'); close the ball of the left foot to Fifth Rear Position, extending the right foot to Fourth Intermediate Aerial Position (count '2'); spring on the right foot along the line of travel bringing the left foot to Third Rear Aerial Position (count '3'); hop RF with slight forward travel, executing a Round-the-Leg movement with LF to Third Aerial Position (count '4').

Note.—On the first two counts the body is at an angle of 45° to the line of travel with the right shoulder leading; on the third count, the body faces the line of travel; on the fourth count, the body is at an angle of 45° to the line of travel with the left shoulder leading.

The movement may be executed with the opposite foot.

The head is always directed along the line of travel.

Progressive Reel Movement

Hop on the left foot taking the right foot to Third Aerial Position, then step with the right foot along the line of travel to Fourth Intermediate Position (count '& 1'); close the ball of the left foot to Third or Fifth Rear Position then step with the right foot along the line of travel (count '& 2').

BASIC STEPS

The movement may be executed with the opposite foot.

Note.—The body is used as for the Progressive Strathspey Movement, beginning to change the shoulder lead on the step which precedes the hop.

C. Basic Steps

A Basic Step is a combination of Basic Movements.

A detailed description of the steps which may be used in Championship Highland Dances is given in Chapter Two.

CHAPTER TWO

Highland Dances

A Dance is a combination of a number of Basic Steps. In the following descriptions of the Dances the following abbreviations are used:

RF=Right foot.   LF=Left foot.

All dances should be preceded by an introduction of four bars of music except when the Reel of Tulloch is performed as a separate dance in which case it has an eight-bar introduction. Consequently there are sixteen counts in the introduction to each Highland Dance, the dancers standing during the first eight counts and bowing during the second eight.

With reference to foot work only, where Fifth Position is used in describing a step in any dance, Third Position may be substituted but, throughout that step, the same position—Third or Fifth—should be used.

In each of the following dances, the first and last steps given should always be performed as such, an exception being the Seann Triubhas, in which any of the quick steps may be used as a last step. The other steps may be performed in a different numerical order to that given in this book.

As a signal for the piper to change from slow to quick tempo the dancer may clap hands on the last beat of the slow step.

1   THE HIGHLAND FLING

A Solo Dance consisting normally of six or eight steps danced without travel except where specially mentioned in the alternatives to the Sixth (Cross-over) Step.

MUSIC: 'Monymusk' or any other suitable Strathspey tune.

Tempo: ♩ =136 (or 34 bars to the minute).

The working foot is never placed in Fourth Position during the dance. The arms, when changing from one position to another, arrive at the new position on the first beat of the bar, except where specially mentioned in the Sixth (Cross-over) Step.

Note.—In the following description, the beginning of each step is given on the assumption that the steps are being performed in the numerical order given, but, should the order be varied, the movement with which each step begins (Hop or Spring) is determined by the finishing position of the preceding step.

Introduction

Bars 1 and 2—Stand as for Bow.

Bars 3 and 4—Bow (count '1, 2, 3, 4, 5, 6'); rise on balls of feet, taking *arms* to First Position on the seventh count, if not already so placed (count '7, 8').

THE HIGHLAND FLING

First Step—Shedding

Bar 1—Commencing with disassemble on to LF, execute the Shedding movement with RF (count '1, 2, 3, 4').

Bar 2—Beginning with spring RF (instead of disassemble), repeat Bar 1 with the other foot (count '5, 6, 7, 8').

Bar 3—Beginning with spring LF (instead of disassemble), repeat Bar 1 (count '1, 2, 3, 4').

Bar 4—Beginning with spring RF, execute the Shedding movement with LF but make a complete turn to the right while executing the three Hops (count '5, 6, 7, 8').

Arms

Second Position in Bars 1, 2 and 3; First or Second Position in Bar 4.

Bars 5 to 8—Beginning with hop RF (instead of disassemble), repeat Bars 1 to 4 with the opposite foot, turning to the left on Bar 8.

Second Step—First Back-Stepping

Bar 1—Hop LF, pointing RF in Second Position (count '1'); hop LF, taking RF to Third Rear Aerial Position (count '2'); hop LF, pointing RF in Second Position (count '3'); hop LF, taking RF to Third Aerial Position (count '4').

Bar 2—Execute back-stepping, springing RF, LF, RF, LF (count '5, 6, 7, 8').

Arms

Second Position in Bar 1; Third Position in Bar 2.

Bars 3 and 4—Beginning with Spring (instead of Hop), repeat Bars 1 and 2 with the opposite foot.

Bars 5 to 8—Beginning with Spring (instead of Hop), repeat Bars 1 to 4.

Third Step—Toe-and-Heel

Bar 1—Commencing with spring LF, execute the Shedding movement with RF (count '1, 2, 3, 4').

Bar 2—Spring, then hop on RF, executing Toe-and-Heel movement with LF in Fifth Position count '5, 6'); spring, then hop on LF, executing Toe-and-Heel movement with RF in Fifth Position (count '7, 8').

Bar 3—Repeat Bar 2 (count '1, 2, 3, 4').

Bar 4—Turn to the right as in Bar 4 of the First Step (count '5, 6, 7, 8').

Arms

Second Position in Bar 1; First Position in Bars 2 and 3; First or Second Position in Bar 4.

Bars 5 to 8—Beginning with Hop (instead of Spring) repeat Bars 1 to 4 with the opposite foot, turning to the left on Bar 8.

Fourth Step—Rocking

Bar 1—Hop LF, pointing RF in Second Position (count '1'); hop LF, taking RF to Third Rear Aerial Position (count '2'); hop LF, pointing RF in Fifth Position then hop LF, extending RF with Shake to Fourth Intermediate Aerial Position (count '3 and [and] a 4' or '3 [and] and a 4').

Bar 2—Execute four Rocks, beginning with spring RF (count '5, 6, 7, 8').

Arms

Second Position in Bar 1; Third Position in Bar 2.

Bars 3 and 4—Beginning with Spring (instead of Hop), repeat Bars 1 and 2 with the opposite foot.

Bars 5 to 8—Beginning with Spring (instead of Hop), repeat Bars 1 to 4.

Fifth Step—Second Back-Stepping

Bar 1—Spring LF, pointing RF in Second Position (count '1'); hop LF, taking RF to Third Rear Aerial Position (count '2'); execute a quick Round-the-Leg movement with RF to Third Aerial Position, then hop LF, extending RF to Fourth Intermediate Aerial Position (count '&3'); hop LF, returning RF to Third Aerial Position (count '4').

Note.—The Round-the-Leg movement with the RF may be executed quickly following the count of '2' in which case the counting for the Bar becomes '1, 2& 3, 4'.

Bar 2—Execute back-stepping, springing RF, LF, RF, LF (count '5, 6, 7, 8').

Arms

Second Position in Bar 1; Third Position in Bar 2.

Bars 3 and 4—Repeat Bars 1 and 2 with opposite foot.

Bars 5 to 8—Repeat Bars 1 to 4.

ALTERNATIVE METHOD

Bar 1—Spring LF, extending RF to Fourth Intermediate Aerial Position (count '1'); hop LF, executing a High Cut in front with RF (count '2&'); hop LF, extending RF to Fourth Intermediate Aerial Position (count '3'); hop LF, returning to Third Aerial Position (count '4').

Bar 2—Execute back-stepping, springing RF, LF, RF, LF (count '5, 6, 7, 8').

Arms

Second Position in Bar 1; Third Position in Bar 2.

Bars 3 and 4—Repeat Bars 1 and 2 with the opposite foot.

Bars 5 to 8—Repeat Bars 1 to 4.

Sixth Step—Cross-over

Bar 1—Execute the Shedding movement with RF (count '1, 2, 3, 4').

Bar 2—Hop LF, pointing RF in Second Position (count '5'); hop LF, taking RF to Third Rear Aerial Position (count '6'); softly passing RF through Third Aerial Position and down in front of the supporting leg, spring on to that foot to displace the LF which is raised to Third Rear Aerial Position (count '7'); hop RF, pointing LF in Fifth Position (count '8').

Arms

Second Position, changing to Second Position on the other side on the count of '7'.

Bars 3 and 4—Repeat Bars 1 and 2 with the opposite foot.

Bars 5 to 8—Repeat Bars 1 to 4.

Note.—In the following three alternative methods given for executing Bar 2 in the above Step, the same *arm* movements are used as those given above.

FIRST ALTERNATIVE METHOD

As for Bar 2 above but simultaneously on landing from the Spring with RF on the count of '7', extend the LF to Second Aerial Position Low.

Note.—A slight lateral travel may be introduced by springing to Third Crossed Position instead of displacing the other foot on the seventh count.

SECOND ALTERNATIVE METHOD

Hop LF, pointing RF in Second Position (count '5'); pause (count '6'); hop LF, taking RF inwards through Third Aerial Position and down in front of the supporting leg to spring on to it in Third Crossed Position, simultaneously extending LF to Second Aerial Position Low (count '&7'); hop RF, pointing LF in Fifth Position (count '8').

THIRD ALTERNATIVE METHOD

Hop LF, pointing RF in Second Position (count '5'); hop LF, executing a Shake action with RF in Second Aerial Position (count '&6'); spring RF in Third Crossed Position, then hop RF pointing LF in Fifth Position (count '7, 8').

Seventh Step—Shake and Turn

Bar 1—Execute Bar 1 of the Fourth Step (Point and Shake).

Bar 2—Turn to right as in Bar 4 of the First Step.

Arms

Second Position in Bar 1; First or Second Position in Bar 2.

Bars 3 and 4—Repeat Bars 1 and 2 with the opposite foot.

Bars 5 to 8—Repeat Bars 1 to 4.

ALTERNATIVE SEVENTH STEP (Double Shake and Rock)

Bar 1—Beginning with hop LF (instead of disassemble), execute Shedding with RF, as in Bar 1 of the First Step (count '1, 2, 3, 4').

Bar 2—Hop LF, pointing RF in Fifth Position then hop LF, extending RF with shake to Fourth Intermediate Aerial Position (count '5 and [and] a 6' or '5 [and] and a 6'); repeat (count '7 and [and] a 8' or '7 [and] and a 8').

Bar 3—Execute four Rocks as in Bar 2 of the Fourth Step (count '1, 2, 3, 4').

Bar 4—Turn to the right as in Bar 4 of the First Step (count '5, 6, 7, 8').

Arms

Second Position in Bars 1 and 2; Third Position in Bar 3; First or Second Position in Bar 4.

Bars 5 to 8—Repeat Bars 1 to 4 with the opposite foot, turning to the left in Bar 8.

Eighth Step—Last Shedding

Bar 1—Beginning with hop LF (instead of disassemble) execute the Shedding movement with RF (count '1, 2, 3, 4').

Bars 2 and 3—Repeat Bar 1 twice (count '5, 6, 7, 8, 1, 2, 3, 4').

Bar 4—Turn to the right as in Bar 4 of the First Step (count '5, 6, 7, 8').

Arms

Second Position in Bars 1, 2 and 3: First or Second Position in Bar 4.

Bar 5—Execute Bar 5 of the First Step—Shedding with LF (count '1, 2, 3, 4').

Bar 6—Repeat Bar 5 (count '5, 6, 7, 8').

Bar 7—Turn to the left as in Bar 8 of the First Step (count '1, 2, 3, 4').

Bar 8—Repeat Bar 7 (count '5, 6, 7, 8').

Arms

Second Position of Bars 5 and 6; First or Second Position in Bars 7 and 8.

ALTERNATIVE LAST SHEDDING

Bars 1 to 6—As for above (Shedding three times with RF, then turn; Shedding twice with LF).

Bar 7—Repeat Bar 6 (Shedding with LF).

Bar 8—Turn to the left as in Bar 8 of the First Step.

FINISH

Step to the right with RF and close LF to First Position (flat) and bow.

2 THE SWORD DANCE (GILLIE CHALIUM)

A solo dance consisting of not more than five or six steps, the last of which is danced to a quick tempo but, when at least five steps are used, the second last step may also be danced to a quick tempo.

MUSIC: 'Gillie Chalium'

Tempo 1 (Slow): $\quad \downarrow$ =128 (or 32 bars to the minute)

Tempo 2 (Quick): $\quad \downarrow$ =168 (or 42 bars to the minute)

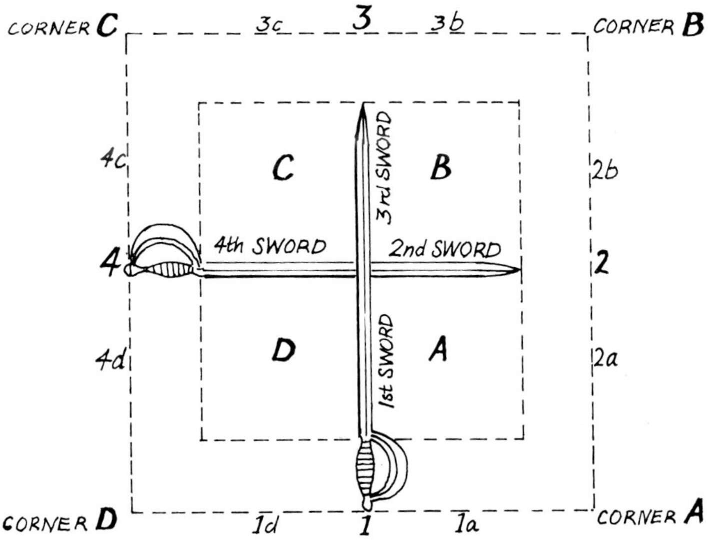

CORNER *C* ___ 3c __ **3** __ 3b ___ CORNER *B*

4c   *C*   3rd SWORD   *B*   2b

4   4th SWORD   2nd SWORD   2

4d   *D*   1st SWORD   *A*   2a

CORNER *D*   1d __ **1** __ 1a   CORNER *A*

The dance is performed round and over two Highland broadswords placed crosswise on the ground at right angles to each other. The top sword is in a direct line from front to back with the hilt (called the top hilt) towards the dancer and with the centre of its blade directly above the centre of the blade of the other sword, the hilt of which is to the dancer's left. The hilts are placed as shown in the diagram but, when broadswords with a certain type of hilt are used, it may be found impracticable to place the hilt of the 'cross' sword as shown so that, in such cases only, that hilt may be placed facing the opposite direction.

Although only two swords are used it has been found expedient to refer to the half blade nearest the dancer's starting place (near the top hilt) as the First Sword then, working in an anticlockwise direction, referring to the other half blades as the Second, Third and Fourth Swords.

In the diagram, two squares (an inner and an outer) are shown by dotted lines. The inner square embraces the sword blades which divide the square into four smaller squares termed 'spaces', the space on the right-hand side of the First Sword being denoted by the letter *A* and the other spaces, working in an anti-clockwise direction, by the letters *B*, *C* and *D*.

In the diagram, the spot on the ground approximately one foot-length from the top hilt and directly in line with the First Sword is denoted by the number *1*, the corresponding spots on the ground in relation to the two sword points and the other hilt being denoted by the

37

appropriate numbers. An outer square is depicted passing through the four spots and the corners are denoted by the letter corresponding to the adjacent space. To the right of spot *1*, on the outer square and directly in front of the centre of space *A*, is the auxiliary spot *1a* and the auxiliary spot *1d* is to the left of spot *1* directly in front of the centre of space *D*. Similarly, the corresponding auxiliary spots in relation to the other main spots are denoted by the appropriate numbers and auxiliary letters.

Note 1.—While dancing over or across the swords the head may be slightly inclined to allow the dancer to see the swords.

Note 2.—When 'inside' the swords, the dancer should be placed in the centre of the space in which he is dancing or should be aiming to land in the centre of the space into which he is moving.

Note 3.—When executing a Pas de Basque 'inside' the swords, there is no extension at the end.

Note 4.—Where Open Bas de Basque and Spring Point are mentioned in the description of the following steps, the supporting foot is given first.

Note 5.—The amount of turn at the end of each step is determined by the starting position of the step which is to follow.

Tempo 1

Introduction

Bars 1 and 2—Stand at 1 as for the Bow.

Bars 3 and 4—Bow (count '1, 2, 3, 4'); step to *1d* with LF and point RF in Third Position, (taking the *arms* to First Position if not already so placed (count '5, 6, 7'); pause (count '8').

Note.—The dancer may rise on the ball of LF on the count of '8'.

First Step—Addressing the Swords

Bar 1—Pas de Basque with RF to *1a* (count '1& 2'); Pas de Basque with LF to *1d* (count '3& 4').

Bar 2—Make three-quarters of a turn to the right with two Pas de Basque, the first with RF to Corner *A*, the second with LF at Corner *A* without travel (count '5& 6, 7& 8').

Bar 3—Pas de Basque with RF to slightly beyond 2 (count '1& 2'); travelling slightly to the left, assemble at 2 with RF in Fifth Position count '3'); disassemble on to LF, executing a High Cut with RF (count '4&').

Bar 4—Execute four High Cuts at 2, springing RF, LF, RF, LF (count '5& 6& 7& 8&').

Arms

First Position in Bars 1, 2 and 3, changing to Third Position on the fourth count of Bar 3; Third Position in Bar 4.

Note.—Where Baby, Beginner or Novice sections are concerned, the dancer may omit the Assemble and Disassemble with High Cut as described in Bar 3 above and substitute a Pas de Basque with LF to 2 (count '3& 4') in which case the *arms* are retained in First Position for that Pas de Basque then raised to Third Position for Bar 4.

THE SWORD DANCE

Bars 5 to 8—As for Bars 1 to 4, starting at 2 and finishing at 3.

Bars 9 to 12—As above, starting at 3 and finishing at 4.

Bars 13 to 16—As above, starting at 4 and finishing at 1.

Second Step—Open Pas de Basque

Bar 1—Pas de Basque into *A* with RF (count '1& 2'); Pas de Basque into *D* with LF (count '3& 4').

Bar 2—Open Pas de Basque into *A* with RF, LF Fourth-opposite-Fifth Position in *B* (count '5& 6'); Open Pas de Basque into *D* with LF, RF Fourth-opposite-Fifth Position in *C* (count '7& 8').

Bar 3—Repeat Bar 2 (count '1& 2, 3& 4').

Bar 4—Execute four Spring Points turning over the Second Sword—RF in *A*, LF Fourth Position in *B* (count '5'); with half turn to right, LF in *B*, RF Fourth Position in *A* (count '6'); with one-eighth turn to right, RF in *B*, LF Fourth Intermediate Position in *A* (count '7'); with one-eighth turn to right, LF in *A*, RF Second Position in *B* (count '8').

Arms

First Position in Bar 1; Third Position in Bars 2 and 3; First Position in Bar 4.

Bars 5 to 8—As for Bars 1 to 4, finishing with the Spring Points turning over the Third Sword.

Bars 9 to 12—As for Bars 1 to 4, finishing with the Spring Points turning over the Fourth Sword.

Bars 13 to 16—As for Bars 1 to 4, finishing with the Spring Points turning over the First Sword.

Note.—If the third (Toe-and-Heel) Step or the Seventh (Quick) or Eighth (Quick) Step with the Alternative Method for the First Bar is to follow, then, on the last Spring Point in Bar 16, make three-eighths turn to the right finishing LF in *D*, RF Fourth Position in *A*.

Third Step—Toe-and-Heel

Begun with the dancer facing *A* with LF (supporting foot) in *D*, RF pointed in Fifth Position or pointed in Fourth Position in *A*.

Bar 1—Spring, then three hops RF in *D*, while executing the Toe-and-Heel movement twice with the working foot (LF) Fourth-opposite-Fifth Position in *A* (count '1, 2, 3, 4').

Bar 2—Repeat Bar 1 reversing the positions of the feet (count '5, 6, 7, 8').

Bar 3—With quarter turn to left on the first count, spring into *A* with RF, then hop RF in *A*, executing one Toe-and-Heel movement with LF in Fifth Position (count '1, 2'); spring, then hop LF in *A*, executing one Toe-and-Heel movement with RF in Fifth Position (count '3, 4').

Bar 4—Execute four Spring Points over the Second Sword, each with the supporting foot in *A* and the working foot Fourth Position in *B* (count '5, 6, 7, 8').

39

Arms

Second Position (R arm up) in Bar 1; Second Position (L arm up) in Bar 2; First Position in Bar 3; Third Position in Bar 4.

Bars 5 to 8—As for Bars 1 to 4, finishing over the Third Sword.

Bars 9 to 12—As for Bars 1 to 4, finishing over the Fourth Sword.

Bars 13 and 14—As for Bars 1 and 2 (over the Fourth Sword).

Bar 15—Travelling straight forward in a line parallel to the First Sword and commencing to turn to the right, Pas de Basque with RF to *1d* (count '1& 2'); assemble at *1d* completing a half turn to finish facing the Fourth Sword with RF in Fifth Position (count '3'); dis-assemble on to LF with High Cut RF (count '4&').

Bar 16—Travelling to the right on the first Spring, execute four High Cuts at *1*, springing RF, LF, RF, LF (count '5& 6& 7& 8&').

FIRST ALTERNATIVE METHOD (*For Bars 15 and 16*)

Bar 15—As for Bar 3, but in *D*.

Bar 16—Execute four Spring Points over the First Sword, turning as described for Bar 16 of the Second Step.

Note.—The Note to the Second Step applies with reference to the Seventh and Eighth (Quick) Steps.

SECOND ALTERNATIVE METHOD (*For Bars 15 and 16*)

To be used only as a lead into the Seventh or Eighth (Quick) Step started by using the alternative method of executing Bar 1.

Bars 15 and 16—As for Bars 3 and 4, finishing over the First Sword.

Fourth Step—Pointing

Bar 1—Pas de Basque into *A* with RF (count '1& 2'); Pas de Basque into *D* with LF (count '3& 4').

Bar 2—Spring Point with RF in *A*, LF Second Position in *D* (count '5'); hop RF, pointing LF in Fifth Position (count '6'); hop RF, pointing LF Fourth Position in *B* (count '7'); hop RF, bringing LF back to point it in Fifth Position (count '8').

Bar 3—Spring Point with LF in *D*, RF Second Position in *A* (count '1'); hop LF, pointing RF in Fifth Position (count '2'); hop LF, pointing RF Fourth Position in *C* (count '3'); hop LF, bringing RF back to point it in Fifth Position (count '4').

Bar 4—Spring Point with RF in *A*, LF Second Position in *D* (count '5'); with quarter turn to left, hop RF pointing LF in Fifth Position (count '6'); Spring Point with LF in *A*, RF Second Position in *B* (count '7'); hop LF, bringing RF back to point it in Fifth Position (count '8').

THE SWORD DANCE

Arms

First Position in Bar 1; to Second Position on count '5' in Bar 2, changing them to Second Position on the other side on count '1' in Bar 3; First Position in Bar 4 or, alternatively, Second Position (right arm raised), changing to Second Position on the other side on count '7'.

Bars 5 to 8—As for Bars 1 to 4 finishing in *B*.

Bars 9 to 12—As for Bars 1 to 4 finishing in *C*.

Bars 13 to 16—As for Bars 1 to 4 finishing in *D*.

Note.—If this Step is to be followed by the Third Step or by the Seventh or Eighth Step with the Alternative Method for the First Bar, then Bar 16 should be executed as follows: Spring Point into *D* with RF, LF Second Position in *C* (count '5'); hop RF, pointing LF in Fifth Position (count '6'); Spring Point with LF in *D*, RF Fourth Position in *A* (count '7'); hop LF, bringing RF back to point it in Fifth Position (count '8').

Fifth Step—Diagonal Points

Bar 1—Pas de Basque in *A* with RF, then into *D* with LF as in Bar 1 of the Fourth Step (count '1& 2, 3& 4').

Bar 2—Open Pas de Basque into *A* with RF, LF Fourth-opposite-Fifth Position in *B* (count '5& 6'); Spring Point with LF in *D*, RF Fourth Intermediate Position in *B* (count '7'); Spring Point with RF in *A*, LF Fourth Intermediate Position in *C* (count '8').

Bar 3—Open Pas de Basque into *D* with LF, RF Fourth-opposite-Fifth Position in *C* (count '1& 2'); Spring Point with RF in *A*, LF Fourth Intermediate Position in *C* (count '3'); Spring Point with LF in *D*, RF Fourth Intermediate Position in *B* (count '4').

Bar 4—Beginning with Spring into *A* with RF, execute four Spring Points turning over the Second Sword as in Bar 4 of the Second Step (count '5, 6, 7, 8').

Arms

First Position in Bar 1; Third Position in Bars 2 and 3; First Position in Bar 4.

Bars 5 to 8—As for Bars 1 to 4 finishing with the Sprint Points turning over the Third Sword.

Bars 9 to 12—As for Bars 1 to 4 finishing with the Spring Points turning over the Fourth Sword.

Bars 13 to 16—As for Bars 1 to 4 finishing with the Spring Points turning over the First Sword.

Note.—The Note to the Second Step applies also to this Step.

Sixth Step—Reverse Points

Bar 1—Pas de Basque into *A* with RF, then into *D* with LF, as in Bar 1 of the Fourth Step (count '1& 2, 3& 4').

Bar 2—Spring Point with RF in *A*, LF Fourth Intermediate Position in *C* (count '5'); with quarter turn to the right, Spring Point with LF in *C*, RF Fourth Intermediate Position in *A*

41

(count '6'); with one-eighth turn to the right, Spring Point with RF in C, LF Fourth Intermediate Position in B (count '7'); with one-eighth turn to the right, Spring Point with LF in B, RF Second Position in C (count '8').

Bar 3—Open Pas de Basque with RF in C, LF in D (count '1& 2'); making a half turn to the right, Open Pas de Basque with LF in D, RF in C (count '3& 4').

Bar 4—Starting with Spring into A on RF, execute four Spring Points turning over the Second Sword as in Bar 4 of the Second Step (count '5, 6, 7, 8').

Arms

First Position in Bar 1; Third Position in Bars 2 and 3; First Position in Bar 4.

Bars 5 to 8—As for Bars 1 to 4 finishing with the Spring Points turning over the Third Sword.

Bars 9 to 12—As for Bars 1 to 4 finishing with the Spring Points turning over the Fourth Sword.

Bars 13 to 16—As for Bars 1 to 4 finishing with the Spring Points turning over the First Sword.

Note.—The note to the Second Step applies also to this step.

MUSIC CHANGES TO TEMPO 2

Seventh Step—Open Pas de Basque Quick-Step

Bar 1—Pas de Basque into A with RF (count '1& 2'); Pas de Basque into D with LF (count '3& 4').

Bar 2—Open Pas de Basque into A with RF, LF Fourth-opposite-Fifth Position in B (count '5& 6'); Open Pas de Basque with LF in A, RF Fourth-opposite-Fifth Position in B (count '7& 8').

Bar 3—With quarter turn to the left on the first count, Open Pas de Basque into B with RF, LF Fourth-opposite-Fifth Position in C (count '1& 2'); Open Pas de Basque with LF in B, RF Fourth-opposite-Fifth Position in C (count '3& 4').

Bar 4—Open Pas de Basque with RF in B, LF Fourth Intermediate Position in D (count '5& 6'); Open Pas de Basque into A with LF, RF Fourth Intermediate Position in C (count '7& 8').

Bar 5—Open Pas de Basque into B with RF, LF Fourth-opposite-Fifth Position in C (count '1& 2'); Open Pas de Basque with LF in B, RF Fourth-opposite-Fifth Position in C (count '3& 4').

Bar 6—With quarter turn to the left on the Fifth Count, Open Pas de Basque into C with RF, LF Fourth-opposite-Fifth Position in D (count '5& 6'); Open Pas de Basque with LF in C, RF Fourth-opposite-Fifth Position in D (count '7& 8').

Bar 7—With quarter turn to the left on the First Count, Open Pas de Basque into D with RF, LF Fourth-opposite-Fifth Position in A (count '1& 2'); Open Pas de Basque with LF in D, RF Fourth-opposite-Fifth Position in A (count '3& 4').

Bar 8—Open Pas de Basque with RF in D, LF Fourth Intermediate Position in B (count '5& 6'); Open Pas de Basque into C with LF, RF Fourth Intermediate Position in A (count '7& 8').

THE SWORD DANCE

Bar 9—Open Pas de Basque with RF into *D*, LF Fourth-opposite-Fifth Position in *A* (count '1& 2'); Open Pas de Basque with LF in *D*, RF Fourth-opposite-Fifth Position in *A* (count '3& 4').

Bars 10 to 16—With a quarter turn to the left on the first count repeat Bars 2 to 8.

Arms

First Position in Bar 1; Third Position in Bars 2 to 16.

ALTERNATIVE METHOD (For Bar 1)

Open Pas de Basque with RF in *D*, LF Fourth-opposite-Fifth Position in *A* (count '1& 2'); Open Pas de Basque with LF in *D*, RF Fourth-opposite-Fifth Position in *A* (count '3& 4').

Arms

Third Position.

It is now necessary to make a quarter turn to the left on beginning Bar 2.

Note.—If the Dance is to finish with this step, Bar 16 should be executed as follows:
Execute four Back-steps in *D*, springing RF, LF, RF, LF, travelling backwards in a curving line to *1d* and taking *arms* down to First Position.

Eighth Step—Crossing and Pointing Quick-Step

Note.—The amount of turn given for any Open Pas de Basque or Spring Point in this step is approximate.

Bar 1—Pas de Basque into *A* with RF (count '&1 2'); Pas de Basque into *D* with LF (count '3& 4').

Bar 2—With one-eighth turn to the left, Open Pas de Basque into *A* with RF, LF Fourth Position in *C* (count '5& 6'); with one-eighth turn to the left, Open Pas de Basque with LF in *A*, RF Second Position in *B* (count '7& 8').

Bar 3—With one-eighth turn to the left, Open Pas de Basque into *B* with RF, LF Fourth Position in *D* (count '1& 2'); with one-eighth turn to the left, Open Pas de Basque with LF in *B*, RF Second Position in *C* (count '3& 4').

Bar 4—With one-eighth turn to the left, Spring Point with RF in *C*, LF Fourth Position in *A* (count '5'); with three-eighths turn to the right, Spring Point with LF in *A*, RF Fourth Intermediate Position in *C* (count '6'); with one-eighth turn to the right, Spring Point with RF in *A*, LF Fourth Intermediate Position in *D* (count '7'); with one-eighth turn to the right, Spring Point with LF in *D*, RF Second Position in *A* (count '8').

Arms

First Position in Bar 1; Third Position in Bars 2 and 3; First Position in Bar 4.

Bars 5 and 6—Repeat Bars 2 and 3 (count '1& 2, 3& 4, 5& 6, 7& 8').

Bar 7—With one-eighth turn to the left, Open Pas de Basque with RF in *C*, LF Fourth-opposite-Fifth Position in *A* (count '1& 2'); with one-eighth turn to the left, Open Pas de Basque with LF in *C*, RF Second Position in *D* (count '3& 4').

Bar 8—With one-eighth turn to the left, Spring Point with RF in *D*, LF Fourth Position in *B* (count '5'); with three-eighths turn to the right, Spring Point with LF in *B*, RF Fourth Intermediate Position in *D* (count '6'); with one-eighth turn to the right, Spring Point with RF in *B*, LF Fourth Intermediate Position in *A* (count '7'); with one-eighth turn to the right, Spring Point with LF in *A*, RF Second Position in *B* (count '8').

Arms

Third Position in Bars 5, 6 and 7; First Position in Bar 8.

Bars 9 to 12—As for Bars 5 to 8, but begin over the Second Sword and finish over the Third Sword.

Bars 13 to 15—As for Bars 9, 10 and 11, but begin over the Third Sword and finish over the Second Sword.

Bar 16—With one-eighth turn to the left, Spring Point with RF in *B*, LF Fourth Position in *D* (count '5'); with three-eighths turn to the right, Spring Point with LF in *D*, RF Fourth Intermediate Position in *B* (count '6'); travelling backwards towards *1d* spring RF, taking LF quickly to Third Aerial Position (count '7'); execute one Back-step springing LF and finishing at *1d* facing the front (count '8').

Arms

First Position in Bar 16.

ALTERNATIVE METHOD (*For Bar 1*)

Open Pas de Basque with RF in *D*, LF Fourth-opposite-Fifth Position in *A* (count '1& 2'); Open Pas de Basque with LF in *D*, RF in *A*, making a quarter-turn to the left to finish with RF in Second Position (count '3& 4').

Arms

Third Position

Note.—When both quick-steps are being danced, this method must be used to begin the last one.

FINISH

Step to 1 with RF and close LF to RF in First Position (flat) and bow.

Note.—In major competitions, if only one quick-step is required, the Eighth Step should be danced.

3 SEANN TRIUBHAS

A Solo Dance consisting normally of not more than eight or ten steps, the last two of which are danced to the quicker tempo.

MUSIC: 'Whistle ower the Lave o't'

Tempo 1 (Slow): ♩=104 (or 26 bars to the minute).

Tempo 2 (Quick): ♩=136 (or 34 bars to the minute).

Grace of movement of body and limbs, associated with precision in foot positions, is a characteristic of this dance. The full range of arm movements is employed with the steps in slower tempo, and the general impression given should be a graceful and flowing exposition of Highland Dancing.

In any Seann Triubhas Step (or alternative method of performing same) where Shuffles are executed only as a 'Four-Shuffle-Break' in the 4th and 8th Bars, the first Shuffle in Bar 4 should commence with spring or hop LF and the first Shuffle in Bar 8 with spring or hop RF.

LINKING OF STEPS

The First Step (Brushing) is invariably followed by the Second Step (Side Travel) and details as to how they are linked together are given in the dance description.

According to the step which is to follow, the finish of the last (8th) bar of certain steps in the slower tempo is varied as detailed below from the method described in the dance description.

(*a*) *When a step which finishes with a Shuffle is to be followed*—

 (i) by any step other than the Sixth Step (Leap and High Cut), the Sixth Alternative Step (Leap and Shedding) or the Eighth Step (Side Heel and Toe) then the extension of the working foot (RF) at the end of that Shuffle, i.e. at the finish of the step, is to Fourth Intermediate Aerial Position.

 (ii) by a step started with a Leap (e.g. the Sixth Step), the last Inward Brush with the RF is finished on the count of '8' with an Assemble with the RF in Fifth Position.

 (iii) by the Eighth Step (Side Heel and Toe), the last Shuffle stops when the RF is brushed inwards to Third Position on the count of '8' then, during the elevation for the Hop with which the Eighth Step starts, the RF is extended towards Second Aerial Position.

(*b*) *When a step which finishes with a Pivot Turn is to be followed*—

 (i) by a step starting with a Hop then for that Hop, a disassemble is substituted.

 (ii) by the Fifth Step (Travelling Balance), then the RF is extended to Fourth Intermediate Aerial Position in preparation for the starting Spring.

(*c*) *When the Fifth Step* (*Travelling Balance*) is to be followed by a step starting with a Leap, the finishing extension of the RF is omitted on the count of '8' and the weight taken on both feet with the RF in Fifth Position.

Note.—The Seventh Step (High Cut in Front and Balance) and the Ninth Step (Double High Cutting) can not be followed by a step starting with a Leap but this does not apply to the Alternative Method for the Seventh Step.

Tempo 1

Introduction

Bars 1 and 2—Stand as for Bow.

Bar 3—Bow (count '1, 2, 3, 4').

Bar 4—Step LF towards Second Position making one-eighth turn to the right, or pivot one-eighth turn to the right taking the weight of the body on LF (flat) (count '5'); step RF to Fourth Rear Position (flat) to finish with LF pointed in Fourth Position (count '6'); stand thus, taking arms to Fifth Position then raise them up in front of the body to Fourth Position and carry them out to Third Position (count '7, 8').

Note.—After the count of '8' there is a slight rise on the ball of the RF in preparation for the start of the First Step.

First Step—Brushing

During the following three bars the dancer travels forward to complete a circle to the left (anti-clockwise), finishing at the starting point facing the front.

Bar 1—Spring LF, then three hops LF, executing an Outward Brush RF with each movement count '1, 2, 3, 4').

Arms

To Fifth Position on count '1' then, with a circular action, take them upwards to Fourth Position and downwards through Third Position on counts '2, 3, 4'.

Bar 2—Spring RF, executing an Outward Brush LF (count '5'); spring LF, executing an Outward Brush RF (count '6'); spring RF, executing an Outward Brush LF (count '7'); spring LF, executing an Outward Brush RF (count '8').

Arms

In First Position, or as for Bar 1.

Bar 3—Spring RF, then three hops RF, executing an Outward Brush LF with each movement (count '1, 2, 3, 4').

Arms

As for Bar 1.

Bar 4—Execute four Shuffles, springing LF, RF, LF, RF (count '5& 6& 7& 8&').

Arms

First Position.

Bars 5 to 8—Starting with Hop instead of Spring, repeat Bars 1 to 4 with the opposite foot but, in Bars 5 to 7, make a circle to the right (clockwise).

Note 1.—When, as is invariably the case, the Second Step (Side Travel) is to follow, the last Shuffle in the 8th Bar finishes with the Inward Brush RF on the count of '8', the extension thereafter being incorporated in the Shake with which the Second Step starts and is counted 'and and a'.

Note 2.—When an Outward Brush is executed in conjunction with a Hop, it is begun by taking the working foot to Third Aerial Position Low during the elevation, and finished with that foot in Fourth Aerial Position. The same also applies when an Outward Brush is executed in conjunction with a Spring, but, in the latter case only, the working foot may be brushed straight forward through First Position to Fourth Aerial Position.

Note 3.—The sequence of Outward Brushes executed with a Hop or Spring in Bars 1 to 3 and Bars 5 to 7 of this step may be varied.

ALTERNATIVE FIRST STEP

Bars 1 to 4—As for Bars 1 to 4 of the First Step but the finishing extension of the LF on the last Shuffle in the 4th Bar is towards Second Aerial Position Low to lead into a Pas de Basque.

Bar 5—Pas de Basque LF (count '1 & 2'); Pas de Basque RF (count '3 & 4').

Arms

First Position.

Bars 6 and 7—Repeat Bar 5 twice more (count '5 & 6, 7 & 8, 1 & 2, 3 & 4').

Bar 8—Hop RF, then three springs LF, RF, LF executing four Shuffles with *arms* in First Position (count '5& 6& 7& 8&').

Note.—Note 1 which follows Bars 5 to 8 of the First Step applies also to this step.

Second Step—Side Travel

Bar 1—Hop LF, extending RF with Shake to Second Aerial Position High (count 'and and a 1'); step on to ball of RF in Fifth Rear Position (count '2'); step LF to Second Position and close ball of RF to Fifth Rear Position or Fifth Position (count '& 3'); step LF to Second Position and close ball of RF to Fifth Rear Position (count '& 4').

During counts '& 3 & 4' the dancer travels directly towards the left side.

Arms

To Fifth Position on count '1' then with a circular action during counts '2 & 3 & 4', take them upwards in front of the body to Fourth Position thence through Third Position and downwards at the sides.

Bar 2—Repeat Bar 1 with the opposite foot, travelling directly towards the right side (count 'and and a 5, 6 & 7 & 8').

Bar 3—Repeat Bar 1 (count 'and and a 1, 2 & 3 & 4').

Bar 4—Execute four Shuffles, springing LF, RF, LF, RF (count '5& 6& 7& 8').

Note.—For the same reason as given in Note 1 under Bars 5 to 8 of the First Step, the last Shuffle in the above bar finishes with the Inward Brush LF on the count of '8'.

Bars 5 to 8—Repeat Bars 1 to 4 with the opposite foot.

Third Step—Diagonal Travel

Bar 1—Facing diagonally to the right, execute the Hop-Brush-Beat-Beat movement with RF (count '1 and [and] a 2'); travelling slightly forward in a diagonal line to the right, spring RF, executing an Outward Brush LF, then spring LF, executing an Outward Brush RF (count '3, 4').

Arms

Second Position for the Hop-Brush-Beat-Beat movement then First or Third Position for the Brushes.

Note.—The remarks in Note 1 to the First Step, concerning an Outward Brush when executed in conjunction with a Spring, apply also to this step.

Bar 2—Execute the Hop-Brush-Brush-Beat movement with RF, finished with or without extension of the working foot on count '6' (count '5 and [and] a 6'); execute a Pivot Turn to the left, finishing facing diagonally to the left (count '7, 8').

Arms

Second Position for the Hop-Brush-Beat-Beat movement, First or Fourth Position during the Pivot Turn. If Fourth Position is used for the turn, the arm which is being raised from First Position is taken up at the side through Third Position.

Bars 3 and 4—Repeat Bars 1 and 2 with the opposite foot, travelling forward in a diagonal line to the left, and turning to the right with the Pivot Turn which is finished facing diagonally to the right.

Bars 5 to 8—Repeat Bars 1 to 4, but finish facing the front.

ALTERNATIVE THIRD STEP

Bar 1—Execute Bar 1 of the Third Step (count '1 and [and] a 2, 3, 4').

Bar 2—Execute the Hop-Brush-Beat-Beat movement with RF finished with or without extension of the working foot on the count of '6' (count '5 and [and] a 6'); making a quarter turn to the left to finish facing diagonally to the left, execute the Shake-Shake-Down movement with RF (count '7 & 8').

Arms

In Second Position, changing to Second Position on the other side on count '8'.

Bars 3 and 4—Repeat Bars 1 and 2 with the opposite foot, and finish facing diagonally to the right.

Bars 5 to 8—Execute Bars 5 to 8 of the Third Step.

Fourth Step—Backward Travel

Bar 1—Execute the Hop-Brush-Beat-Beat movement with RF finished with or without extension of the working foot on the count of '2' (count '1 and [and] a 2'); hop LF, taking RF to Third Rear Aerial Position (count '3'); hop LF, executing a Round-the-Leg movement with RF to Third Aerial Position (count '4').

Arms

Second Position.

Bar 2—Repeat the Hop-Brush-Beat-Beat movement as in Bar 1 (count '5 and [and] a 6'); execute the Shake-Shake-Down movement with RF, finished by extending LF to Fourth Intermediate Aerial Position (count '7 & 8').

Arms

Second Position, changing to Second Position on the other side on count '8'.

Bars 3 and 4—Repeat Bars 1 and 2 with the opposite foot.

Bars 5 to 8—Repeat Bars 1 to 4.

Note.—Whilst executing the Shake-Shake-Down movements in the above step, gradually move backwards so that original position is regained at the end of the step. If not preceded by the Third Step (Diagonal Travel) this step may be performed on the spot, i.e. without travel.

ALTERNATIVE FOURTH STEP

Bar 1—Execute the Hop-Brush-Beat-Beat movement, followed by the Shake-Shake-Down movement as in Bar 2 of the Fourth Step (count '1 and [and] a 2, 3 & 4').

Bar 2—Repeat Bar 1 with the opposite foot (count '5 and [and] a 6, 7 & 8').

Bar 3—Repeat Bar 1 (count '1 and [and] a 2, 3 & 4').

Bar 4—Execute four Shuffles, springing LF, RF, LF, RF (count '5& 6& 7& 8&').

Arms

Second Position in Bars 1, 2 and 3; First Position in Bar 4.

Bars 5 to 8—Repeat Bars 1 to 4 with the opposite foot.

Note.—Whilst executing the Shake-Shake-Down movements in the above step, move gradually backwards so that original position is regained at the end of the step.

Fifth Step—Travelling Balance

Bar 1—Execute the Balance movement, springing RF, LF (count '1, 2'); spring RF to displace LF which is taken to Third Rear Aerial Position (count '3'); execute a Round-the-Leg movement with RF to Third Aerial Position then hop RF, extending LF to Fourth Intermediate Aerial Position (count '3 & 4' or '3 &4').

Arms

Third Position.

Bar 2—Execute the Travelling Balance movement, beginning with LF (count '5 & 6, 7 & 8').

Bars 3 and 4—Repeat Bars 1 and 2 with the opposite foot.

Bars 5 to 8—Repeat Bars 1 to 4.

Note.—If the Sixth Step is to follow, there is no extension of the foot on the last count of the above step, the feet remaining in Fifth Position.

Sixth Step—Leap and High Cut

Note.—This step should follow a step which may be finished with the weight of the body equally distributed on the balls of both feet in Third or Fifth Position.

Bar 1—Leap, landing with RF in front (count '1'); disassemble with High Cut RF (count '2&'); hop LF, executing a High Cut in Front RF (count '3 and [and]'); place RF on the half point in Fifth Position, then lightly beat ball of LF in Fifth Rear Position, extending RF to midway between Fourth Aerial Position Low and Fourth Intermediate Aerial Position Low (count 'a 4');

Bar 2—Execute three Shuffles, springing RF, LF, RF (count '5& 6& 7&'); beginning with LF, execute the elevation as for Shuffle but assemble with RF in front in Fifth Position (count '8').

Arms

Circle arms outwards and upwards at the sides through Third Position to Fourth Position during the Leap on count '1'; Second Position for the remainder of Bar 1; First Position in Bar 2.
     or, alternatively,
First Position during the Leap on count '1' then, during counts '2, 3, 4', raise the arms outwards at the sides through Third Position to Fourth Position; during Bar 2, take the arms outwards through Third Position then downwards at the sides.

Bars 3 and 4—Repeat Bars 1 and 2 with the opposite foot.

Bars 5 to 8—Repeat Bars 1 to 4 but in the last Bar, the third Shuffle is finished with the Inward Brush RF to Third Position on the count of '7' then the RF is placed on the half point towards Fourth Intermediate Position and the LF closed to Fifth Rear Position, simultaneously extending the RF, if required, to the position for starting the next step.

ALTERNATIVE SIXTH STEP (Leap and Shedding)

Bar 1—Leap, landing with LF in front (count '1'); disassemble, taking RF to Third Rear Aerial Position (count '2'); hop LF, executing a Round-the-Leg movement with RF to Third Aerial Position (count '3'); place RF on the half point towards Fourth Intermediate Position, then close ball of LF to Fifth Rear Position extending RF to midway between Fourth Aerial Position Low and Fourth Intermediate Aerial Position Low (count '& 4').

SEANN TRIUBHAS

Arms

First Position on count '1', raise arms up at sides through Third Position to Fourth Position on counts '2, 3 & 4', or alternatively, circle arms upwards and outwards at the sides through Third Position to Fourth Position on count '1'; Second Position on counts '2, 3, 4'.

Bar 2—Execute Bar 2 of the Sixth Step with slight backward travel to regain starting line (count '5& 6& 7& 8').

Arms

On counts '5& 6& 7&' take arms down at sides through Third Position to arrive in First Position on count '8', or alternatively, Second Position during the Bar.

Bars 3 and 4—Repeat Bars 1 and 2 with the opposite foot.

Bars 5 to 8—Repeat Bars 1 to 4 but in the last Bar, the third Shuffle is finished with the Inward Brush RF to Third Position on the count of '7' then the RF is placed on the half point towards Fourth Intermediate Position and the LF closed to Fifth Rear Position, simultaneously extending the RF, if required, to the position for starting the next step.

Seventh Step—High Cut in Front and Balance

Bar 1—Hop LF, with High Cut in front RF (count '1 and [and]'); place RF on the half point in Fifth Position, then lightly beat the ball of LF in Fifth Rear Position, extending RF to Fourth Intermediate Aerial Position (count 'a 2'); execute the Balance movement, springing RF, LF (count '3, 4').

Arms

Second Position on counts '1 and [and] a 2'; Third Position on counts '3, 4'.

Bar 2—Repeat counts '1 and [and] a 2' of Bar 1 (count '5 and [and] a 6'); spring RF, taking LF to Third Rear Aerial Position (count '7'); hop RF executing a Round-the-Leg movement with LF to Third Aerial Position (count '8').

Arms

Second Position on counts '5 and [and] a 6' changing to Second Position on the other side on count '7'.

Bars 3 and 4—Repeat Bars 1 and 2 with the other foot.

Bars 5 to 8—Repeat Bars 1 to 4.

ALTERNATIVE SEVENTH STEP

Bars 1 to 3—Execute Bars 1 to 3 of the Seventh Step.

Bar 4—Execute four Shuffles, springing LF, RF, LF, RF.

51

Bars 5 to 8—Repeat Bars 1 to 4 with the opposite foot.

Note.—Following each High Cut in Front, instead of lowering the working foot to Fifth Position, it may be placed on the half point towards Fourth Intermediate Position and the rear foot closed up to it in Fifth Rear Position. To compensate for the resultant slight forward travel, and to regain line, the dancer travels backwards during the Shuffles in Bars 4 and 8.

Eighth Step—Side Heel-and-Toe

Bar 1—Hop LF, extending RF towards Second Aerial Position during the elevation and taking it inwards to Third Aerial or Third Rear Aerial Position simultaneously on landing (count '1'); place heel of RF towards Second Position, then, momentarily taking the weight on that heel, place the ball of LF in Fifth Rear Position, allowing the knee of the right leg to relax (count '& 2'); place RF on the half point towards Second Position, then place ball of LF in Fifth Rear Position (count '& 3'); place heel of RF towards Second Position then close ball of LF to Fifth Rear Position as before (count '& 4').

Arms

Second Position.

Note.—During this Bar the dancer travels directly towards the right side.

Bar 2—Execute Bar 2 of the Fourth Step (count '5 and [and] a 6, 7 & 8').

Bars 3 and 4—Beginning with hop RF, repeat Bars 1 and 2 with the opposite foot, travelling directly towards the left side back to starting point.

Bars 5 to 8—Beginning with hop LF, repeat Bars 1 to 4 but a Pivot Turn to the left may be executed on counts '7, 8' in Bar 6, in which case a Pivot Turn to the right is executed on counts '7, 8' in Bar 8.

Ninth Step—Double High Cutting

Bar 1—Execute the Hop-Brush-Beat-Beat movement with RF (count '1 and [and] a 2'); hop LF with High Cut RF (count '3&'); hop LF with High Cut in Front RF (count '4&').

Note.—The extension to Second Aerial Position of the working foot incorporated in the High Cut, may be executed either simultaneously on 'beating' the rear foot on the count of '2', or during the elevation for the Hop which follows that count.

Bar 2—Execute the Hop-Brush-Beat-Beat movement with RF but finish with the weight evenly distributed on both feet with the RF in Fifth Position (count '5 and [and] a 6'); disassemble, extending both feet towards Second Aerial Position (as for Leap) during the elevation and land on RF with High Cut LF (count '7&'); hop RF with High Cut in Front LF (count '8&').

Note—When executing the above High Cuts in Front, the extension may be turned towards Second Aerial Position.

52

SEANN TRIUBHAS

Arms

Second Position, changing to the other side on the count of '7'.

Bars 3 and 4—Repeat Bars 1 and 2 with the opposite foot.

Bars 5 to 8—Repeat 1 to 4.

MUSIC CHANGES TO TEMPO 2

Tenth Step—Shedding with Back-Step

Bar 1—Hop LF, pointing RF in Second Position (count '1'); hop LF, taking RF to Third Rear Aerial Position (count '2'); hop LF, executing a Round-the-Leg movement with RF, to Third Aerial Position (count '3'); execute one Back-step with RF (count '4').

Arms

Second Position, changing to the other side on count '4'.

Bar 2—Repeat Bar 1 with the opposite foot (count '5, 6, 7, 8').

Bar 3—Repeat Bar 1 (count '1, 2, 3, 4').

Bar 4—Hop RF, pointing LF in Second Position (count '5'); turn to the right as in Bar 4 of the First Highland Fling Step (count '6, 7, 8').

Bars 5 to 8—Repeat Bars 1 to 4 with the opposite foot and turning to the left on Bar 8.

Eleventh Step—Toe-and-Heel, and Rock

Bar 1—Spring LF, then hop LF (or two hops LF if required), executing the Toe-and-Heel movement in Second Position with RF (count '1, 2'); two hops LF, executing the Toe-and-Heel movement in Fifth Position with RF (count '3, 4').

Arms

Second Position.

Bar 2—Execute four Rocks, springing RF, LF, RF, LF (count '5, 6, 7, 8').

Arms

Third Position.

Bars 3 and 4—Repeat Bars 1 and 2 with the opposite foot.

Bars 5 to 8—Repeat Bars 1 to 4.

Twelfth Step—Pointing and Back-Stepping

Bar 1—Hop (or spring if required) LF, pointing RF midway between Fourth Position and Fourth Intermediate Position (count '1'); hop LF, taking RF to Third Aerial Position (count '2');

53

hop LF, pointing RF midway between Fourth Position and Fourth Intermediate Position (count '3'); spring RF to displace LF which is taken sharply to Third Rear Aerial Position (count '4').

Arms

Second Position, changing to the other side on count 4.

Bar 2—Repeat Bar 1 with the opposite foot (count '5, 6, 7, 8').

Bar 3—Repeat Bar 1 (count '1, 2, 3, 4').

Bar 4—Execute four Back-steps, springing LF, RF, LF, RF (count '5, 6, 7, 8').

Arms

Third Position.

Note.—The Back-stepping in Bar 4 is begun from Third Rear Aerial Position.

Bars 5 to 8—Repeat Bars 1 to 4 with the opposite foot.

Thirteenth Step—Heel-and-Toe and Shedding

Bar 1—Hop (or spring) LF, pointing RF in Second Position (count '1'); hop LF, taking RF to Third Rear Aerial Position (count '2'); execute the Heel-and-Toe movement with RF (count '3, 4').

Bar 2—Beginning with hop, instead of disassemble, execute the Shedding movement with RF (count '5, 6, 7, 8').

Arms

Second Position in Bars 1 and 2.

Bars 3 and 4—Beginning with spring RF, repeat Bars 1 and 2 with the opposite foot.

Bars 5 to 8—Beginning with spring LF, repeat Bars 1 to 4.

Fourteenth Step—Heel-and-Toe, Shedding, and Back-Stepping

Bars 1 and 2—Execute Bars 1 and 2 of the Thirteenth Step.

Bar 3—Execute four Back-steps, springing RF, LF, RF, LF (count '1, 2, 3, 4').

Bar 4—Turn to the right as in Bar 4 of the First Highland Fling Step (count '5, 6, 7, 8').

Arms

Second Position in Bars 1 and 2; Third Position in Bar 3; First or Second Position in Bar 4.

Bars 5 to 8—Repeat Bars 1 to 4 with the opposite foot, turning to the left on Bar 8.

Note.—If the above is used as a last step, Bars 7 and 8 may be executed as follows:

Hop LF, pointing RF in Second Position (count '1'); execute two turns to the left as in Bars 7 and 8 of the Eighth Highland Fling Step (count '2, 3, 4, 5, 6, 7, 8').

54

Fifteenth Step—Back-Stepping

Bar 1—Hop LF, pointing RF in Second Position (count '1'); hop LF, taking RF to Third Rear Aerial Position (count '2'); execute two Back-steps, springing RF, LF, and finish with RF in Third Aerial Position (count '3, 4').

Arms

Second Position on counts '1, 2'; Third Position on counts '3, 4'.

Bar 2—Starting with spring (instead of hop), repeat Bar 1 with the opposite foot (count '5, 6, 7, 8').

Bar 3—Starting with spring (instead of hop), repeat Bar 1 (count '1, 2, 3, 4').

Bar 4—Turn to the right as in the fourth bar of the First Step of the Highland Fling (count '5, 6, 7, 8').

Bars 5 to 8—Repeat Bars 1 to 4 with the opposite foot.

Preparation for the Finish

Method 1

On the last bar of the final step of the Dance assemble with LF in front (count '5'); leap, landing with RF in front (count '6, 7'); pause (count '8').

Method 2

On the fourth count of the seventh bar of the final step of the Dance, assemble with LF in front (count '4'), then execute Bar 8 as follows:
Leap, landing with or without change of foot (count '5, 6'); leap, landing with RF in front (count '7, 8').

Method 3

Execute two turns to the left as in the Eighth Highland Fling Step (see note to Fourteenth Step).

FINISH

Step to the right with RF, then close LF to RF in First Position (flat) and bow.

4 STRATHSPEY

A Dance performed by four Dancers.

MUSIC: Any Strathspey Tune.

Tempo: ♩=136 (or 34 bars to the minute).

A→   ←B   C→   ←D

1 ←— 4'6" —→ 2 ← 3' → 3 ←— 4'6" —→ 4

The Set Line is an imaginary straight line connecting points *1* and *4* thus passing through points *2* and *3*.

As shown in the diagram, the four dancers *A, B, C* and *D* stand on the Set Line at points *1, 2, 3* and *4* respectively, *A* and *B* are facing each other, *C* and *D* are also facing each other.

Introduction

Bars 1 and 2—All stand as for bow (8 counts).

Bar 3—All bow (count '1, 2, 3, 4').

Bar 4—All pivot one-eighth turn to the left on ball of LF, releasing the heel of RF (count '5'); point RF in Fourth Position, taking *arms* to First Position if not already so placed (count '6'); pause (count '7'); rise on ball of LF taking RF to Third Aerial Position and turning the body at 45° to the line of travel for the Figure of Eight and raising the *arms* to Third Position (count '8').

or, alternatively,

Pause, taking *arms* to First Position if not already so placed (count '5, 6, 7'); rise on ball of LF swivelling to the left till the body is at 45° to the line of travel for the Figure of Eight taking RF to Third Aerial Position and taking the *arms* to Third Position (count '8').

First Step

FIGURE OF EIGHT

Bars 1 to 7—Moving forward along the line of travel, as indicated by the arrows in the diagram, each dancer executes seven Progressive Strathspey movements. Dancers *A* and *D* return to their starting positions at points *1* and *4* respectively; *B* and *C*, when approaching each other on the seventh bar, make approximately a three-eighths turn to the right, so that *C* finishes at point *2* facing *A* and *B* at point *3* facing *D*.

Arms

Third Position throughout.

Bar 8—Taking *arms* to First Position, assemble with LF in front (count '5'); leap, landing with RF in front (count '6, 7'); pause (count '8').

Note.—During the Figure of Eight, when *A* and *D* are passing each other in the centre, *B* and *C* are passing through the outer points, and vice versa.

STRATHSPEY

FIRST ALTERNATIVE METHOD (For Bars 7 and 8)

Bar 7—Execute the first three counts of the Strathspey movement with RF (Step, Step, Spring), finished with LF in Third Rear Aerial Position (count '1, 2, 3'); gently extend LF to Second Aerial Position (count '4').

Bar 8—Taking *arms* to First Position, assemble with LF in front (count '5'); Leap, landing with change of foot (count '6, 7'); pause (count '8').

SECOND ALTERNATIVE METHOD (For Bars 7 and 8)

Bar 7—Execute the first three counts of the First Alternative Method above, then execute a Round-the-Leg movement with LF to Third Aerial Position, followed by hop RF, extending LF to Second Aerial Position (count '1, 2, 3 & 4' or '1, 2, 3 &4').

Bar 8—As for Bar 8 in First Alternative above (count '5, 6, 7, 8').

THIRD ALTERNATIVE METHOD (For Bars 7 and 8)

Bar 7—Execute the first three counts of the First Alternative Method above, finished with LF in Third Rear Aerial Position (count '1, 2, 3'); taking *arms* to First Position, assemble with LF in front (count '4').

Bar 8—Leap, landing without change of foot (count '5, 6'); leap, landing with change of foot (count '7, 8').

SETTING

Bars 9 to 16—All dance a Highland Fling Step, e.g. the Fourth (Rocking) Step.

Second Step

FIGURE OF EIGHT

Bars 1 to 8—As for Bars 1 to 8 of the First Step with *B* and *C* finishing in their original positions at points *2* and *3* respectively.

SETTING

Bars 9 to 16—All dance a Highland Fling Step, e.g. the Sixth (Cross-over) Step.

The First Step or the First and Second Steps may be repeated using a different Highland Fling Step each time. The Strathspey is usually followed by a Reel, but if not, all dancers face the front after the last setting step, then bow.

Note 1.—As will be seen from the diagram, with reference to the line of travel, the term 'Figure of Eight' is a misnomer, but the name has been retained because it is traditional.

Note 2.—As it is essential to have the RF in Third Aerial Position to start the Progressive Strathspey movement which is to follow the Highland Fling Step used for Setting, the last (8th) bar of Highland Fling Steps which finish with the following movements must be altered as described below:

BACK-STEPPING. On the last count of the step, hop LF retaining RF in Third Aerial Position.

57

ROCKING. On the last two counts of the step, spring LF, taking RF to Third Rear Aerial Position, then hop LF, executing a Round-the-Leg movement with RF to Third Aerial Position or, alternatively, on the last count of the step, hop LF, taking RF to Third Aerial Position.

CROSS-OVER. On the last count of the step, hop LF, taking RF to Third Aerial Position.

HIGHLAND FLING TURN. Following the completion of the last count of the turn, execute a Round-the-Leg movement with RF to Third Aerial Position. This movement is not sharply executed and, when combined with the forward Step that starts the Progressive Strathspey movement, gives a perfect Half-Beat Rhythm of '& 1'.

Steps most generally used for Setting are 'Rocking', 'Cross-over', 'First or Second Back-Stepping' and 'Double Shake and Rock'.

The above also applies to the last Setting Step when the Strathspey is being followed by a Reel.

Note 3.—If the Strathspey is to be followed by the complete Reel of Tulloch an even number of Strathspey steps should be danced, so that the dancers are in their original position to begin the Reel.

Note 4.—Bar 1 of all Highland Fling Steps used for setting will begin with Disassemble instead of Hop or Spring.

Note 5.—On the last two beats of a Setting step the dancers should make a one-eighth turn to the left preparatory to starting the Figure of Eight.

5 HIGHLAND REEL

This dance usually follows the Strathspey with the music changing to Reel Time without any break between the dances.

MUSIC: Any Scottish Reel Tune.

Tempo: ♩=120 or 60 Bars to the minute (count two in the bar).

Note 1.—During the Highland Reel the distance between the points may be reduced.

Note 2.—On the last two beats of a Setting Step the dancers should make a one-eighth turn to the left preparatory to starting the Figure of Eight. An exception is at the end of the Last Basic Reel Step (High-Cutting).

First Step

FIGURE OF EIGHT

Bars 1 to 8—The dancers follow the same line of travel, and begin and finish at the same points as described in Part 1 of the First Step in the Strathspey, but eight Progressive Reel movements are danced to complete the Figure of Eight.

BASIC REEL STEPS

Arms

Third Position throughout.

or alternatively

Execute seven Progressive Reel movements with *arms* in Third Position (7 bars); assemble with LF in front, taking *arms* to First Position, then change (1 bar).

If this method is used, a Basic Reel Step which is described as beginning with Hop will instead begin with Disassemble and, for a Basic Reel Step described as beginning with Assemble or the Balance movement, preparation is made on the last count of the bar preceding that on which the Basic Reel Step begins, by extending the RF towards Second Aerial Position Low or to Fourth Intermediate Aerial Position.

SETTING

Bars 9 to 16—All dance a Basic Reel Step.

Second Step

FIGURE OF EIGHT

Bars 1 to 8—As for the First Step, but the dancers finish as for the Second Step of the Strathspey.

SETTING

Bars 9 to 16—All dance a Basic Reel Step.

The First, or the First and Second Steps may be repeated using a different Basic Reel Step each time.

When setting for the last time, all dancers execute the Last Basic Reel Step (High-Cutting) to finish facing partners.

FINISH

All step to the right with RF, close LF to RF in First Position (flat) of the feet, then bow to partner. All step with LF into line facing the front, close RF to LF in First Position (flat) of the feet, then bow to audience.

6 BASIC REEL STEPS

First Step—Pas de Basque

This step is performed by dancers *A* and *D* to start the Reel of Tulloch, their starting positions and their line of travel during Bars 1 and 2 being given (*a*) on page 55 when the Reel of Tulloch has been preceded by the Strathspey and (*b*) on page 66 when the dance is being performed by itself.

Bars 1 and 2—Two Pas de Basque RF, LF, travelling forward to finish facing each other on the Set Line with *A* at point *2* and *D* at point *3* (count '1 & 2, 3 & 4').

Note.—The starting Spring for each Pas de Basque is towards Fourth Intermediate Position.

Bars 3 and 4—Two Pas de Basque RF, LF, making a complete turn to the right on the spot (count '5 & 6, 7 & 8').

Bars 5 and 6—Pas de Basque RF, travelled slightly towards Second Position (count '1 & 2'); assemble on the Set Line (*A* at point *2*, *D* at point *3*) with RF in Fifth Position (count '3'); disassemble on to LF with High Cut RF (count '4 &').

Bars 7 and 8—Execute four High Cuts, springing RF, LF, RF, LF (count '5 & 6 & 7 & 8 &').

Arms

First Position, changing to Third Position during the Disassemble with High Cut in Bar 6.

Second Step—Shake and Travel

Bar 1—Hop LF, placing RF on the half point in Fifth Position (count '1'); hop LF, extending RF with Shake as for Highland Fling but to Second Aerial Position (count 'and [and] a 2' or '[and] and a 2').

Bar 2—Hop LF, then step on to RF in Fifth Rear Position (count '&3'); step LF to Second Position, then close ball of RF to Fifth Position (count '& 4').

Arms

Second Position, changing to Second Position on the other side on counts '& 4'.

Bars 3 and 4—Repeat Bars 1 and 2 with the opposite foot (count '5 and [and] a 6 &7 & 8' or '5 [and] and a 6 &7 & 8').

Bars 7 and 8—Execute two High Cuts, springing LF, RF (count 5 & 6 &'); spring LF, taking RF as for High Cut to Third Rear Aerial Position, then execute a Round-the-Leg movement with RF to Third Aerial Position (count '7 &'); hop LF with High Cut RF (count '8 &').

Note.—On counts '7 &', the dancer may execute a High Cut with RF instead of the Round-the-Leg movement described above.

Arms

Third Position.

ALTERNATIVE METHOD

Bars 1 to 4—Execute Bars 1 to 4 as described above.

Bars 5 to 8—Execute eight High Cuts with Spring, beginning with spring RF (count '1 & 2 & 3 & 4 & 5 & 6 & 7 & 8 &').

Arms

Third Position.

BASIC REEL STEPS

Third Step—Balance and Pas de Basque

Bar 1—Execute the Balance movement, springing RF, LF (count '1, 2').

Bar 2—Pas de Basque RF (count '3 & 4').

Arms

Third Position in Bar 1, First Position in Bar 2.

Bars 3 and 4—Repeat Bars 1 and 2 with the opposite foot (count '5, 6, 7 & 8').

Bars 5 to 8—Repeat Bars 1 to 4.

FIRST ALTERNATIVE METHOD

Bars 1 to 6—Execute Bars 1 to 6, as described above.

Bars 7 and 8—Execute Bars 7 and 8 of the First Step.

SECOND ALTERNATIVE METHOD

Bars 1 to 4—Execute Bars 1 to 4 as described above.

Bars 5 to 8—Execute Bars 5 to 8 of the First Step Alternative Method. (8 High Cuts.)

Fourth Step—Brushing

Bar 1—Hop LF, executing an Outward Brush with RF from Third Aerial Position Low to Fourth Aerial Position (count '1'); repeat hop LF, with Outward Brush RF (count '2').

Bar 2—Spring RF, executing an Outward Brush with LF from Third Aerial Position Low to Fourth Aerial Position (count '3'); hop RF, repeating the Outward Brush LF (count '4').

Bars 3 and 4—Execute four High Cuts, springing LF, RF, LF, RF (count '5 & 6 & 7 & 8 &').

Arms

Second Position in Bars 1 and 2; Third Position in Bars 3 and 4.

Bars 5 to 8—Repeat Bars 1 to 4 with the opposite foot.

Fifth Step—High Cuts and Spring Points

Bar 1—Execute two High Cuts, springing RF, LF (count '1 & 2 &').

Bar 2—Execute two Spring Points, springing RF, LF, with the working foot in Fourth Position each time (count '3, 4').

Arms

Third Position in Bar 1; First Position in Bar 2.

Bars 3 to 6—Repeat Bars 1 and 2 twice more (count '5 & 6 & 7, 8, 1 & 2 & 3, 4).

Bars 7 and 8—Execute four High Cuts, springing RF, LF, RF, LF, with arms in Third Position (count '5 & 6 & 7 & 8 &') or, alternatively, repeat Bars 1 and 2 (count '5 & 6 & 7, 8').

Sixth Step—Balance and Round-the-Leg

Bar 1—Execute the Balance movement, springing RF, LF (count '1, 2').

Bar 2—Spring RF, taking LF to Third Rear Aerial Position, execute a Round-the-Leg movement with LF to Third Aerial Position (count '3 &'); hop RF, extending LF to Fourth Intermediate Aerial Position (count '4').

Bars 3 and 4—Repeat Bars 1 and 2 with the opposite foot (count '5, 6, 7 & 8').

Bar 5—Repeat Bar 2 (count '1 & 2').

Bar 6—Repeat Bar 5 with the opposite foot (count '3 & 4').

Bars 7 and 8—Execute four High Cuts as in Bar 8 of the Fourth Step (count '5 & 6 & 7 & 8 &').

Arms
Third Position throughout.

FIRST ALTERNATIVE METHOD
Bars 1 to 4—Execute Bars 1 to 4 as described above.

Bars 5 and 6—Repeat Bars 1 and 2.

Bars 7 and 8—Execute Bars 7 and 8 of the First Step.

SECOND ALTERNATIVE METHOD
Bars 1 to 4—Execute Bars 1 to 4 as described above.

Bars 5 to 8—Execute eight High Cuts (count '1 & 2 & 3 & 4 & 5 & 6 & 7 & 8 &').

Seventh Step—Back-Step and Travel

Bar 1—Take RF sharply to Third Aerial Position and execute one Back-step (count '1'); place LF on the half point towards Second Position (count '&'); place ball of RF in Fifth Rear Position, extending LF to Second Aerial Position (count '2'); take LF to Third Rear Aerial Position (count '&').

Bar 2—Spring LF with High Cut RF (count '3 &'); spring RF, taking LF as for High Cut to Third Rear Aerial Position (count '4'); execute a Round-the-Leg movement with LF to Third Aerial Position (count '&').

Bars 3 and 4—Repeat Bars 1 and 2 with the opposite foot (count '5 & 6 & 7 & 8 &').

Bars 5 to 8—Repeat Bars 1 to 4.

Arms
Third Position throughout.

Eighth Step—Assemble and Travel

Bar 1—Assemble with LF in front (count '1'); disassemble, taking RF to Third Rear Aerial Position (count '2').

BASIC REEL STEPS

Arms

First Position on count '1', Second Position on count '2'.

Bar 2—Hop LF, executing a Round-the-Leg movement with RF to Third Aerial Position (count '3'); place RF on the half point towards Second Position (count '&'); close ball of LF to Fifth Rear Position, extending RF to Second Aerial Position (count '4').

Arms

Second Position.

Bars 3 and 4—Repeat Bars 1 and 2 with the opposite foot (count '5, 6, 7 & 8').

Bars 5 and 6—Repeat Bars 1 and 2 (count '1, 2, 3 & 4').

Bars 7 and 8—Execute four High Cuts springing RF, LF, RF, LF, with *arms* in Third Position (count '5 & 6 & 7 & 8 &').

Ninth Step—High Cut in Front and Balance

Bar 1—Hop LF, with High Cut in Front RF (count '1 and [and]'); place RF on the half point in Fifth Position, then lightly beat the ball of LF in Fifth Rear Position, at the same time extending RF to Fourth Intermediate Aerial Position (count 'a 2').

Arms

Second Position.

Bar 2—Execute the Balance movement, springing RF, LF (count '3, 4').

Arms

Third Position.

Bar 3—Repeat Bar 1 (count '5 and [and] a 6').

Bar 4—Spring RF, taking LF to Third Rear Aerial Position (count '7'); hop RF, executing a Round-the-Leg movement with LF to Third Aerial Position (count '8').

Arms

Second Position.

Bars 5 to 8—Repeat Bars 1 to 4 with the opposite foot.

ALTERNATIVE METHOD

Bars 1 to 6—Execute Bars 1 to 6 as described above.

Bars 7 and 8—Execute Bars 7 and 8 of the First Step. (8 High Cuts.)

Tenth Step—Shuffle

Bar 1—Assemble with RF in front (count '1'); disassemble, taking LF to Third Rear Aerial Position (count '2').

Arms

First Position on count '1', Second Position on count '2'.

Bar 2—Hop RF, executing a Round-the-Leg movement with LF to Third Aerial Position (count '3'); place LF on the half point towards Fourth Intermediate Position, then close ball of RF to Fifth Rear Position, at the same time extending LF to midway between Fourth Aerial Position Low and Fourth Intermediate Aerial Low (count '& 4').

Arms

Second Position.

Bars 3 and 4—Beginning with spring LF, and travelling slightly backwards to regain line, execute four Shuffles with arms in First Position (count '5 & 6 & 7 & 8 &').

Bars 5 to 8—Repeat Bars 1 to 4 with the opposite foot.

Last Step—High Cutting

Bars 1 to 8—Execute sixteen High Cuts, making a gradual complete turn to the right on the spot with *arms* in Third Position.

Note.—It is not necessary to execute the High Cuts with alternate feet. Double High Cutting may be introduced by using a suitable combination of Springs and Hops. Furthermore, a Round-the-Leg movement may be substituted for one of the Double High Cuts. An example (starting with spring RF) is as follows:

Spring, spring, spring, hop; spring, spring, spring, hop; spring, hop, spring, hop; spring, spring, spring, spring.

7 REEL OF TULLOCH OR 'HULLACHAN'

MUSIC: 'Reel of Tulloch'

Tempo: ♩=120 or 60 Bars to the Minute (count two in a bar).

This dance usually follows the Strathspey as an alternative to the Highland Reel, in which case the dancers start in the same position as for the Strathspey, namely *A* and *B* facing each other at points *1* and *2* respectively; *C* and *D* facing each other at points *3* and *4* respectively.

Note.—All High Cuts performed during this dance are executed on the Set Line.

Part 1

Bars 1 to 8—Dancers *A* and *D* dance the First Basic Reel Step (Pas de Basque).

Note.—During Bars 1 and 2 the forward travel is along the same line as for the Figure of Eight in the Strathspey or the Highland Reel.

During Bars 1 and 2 of the above, dancers *B* and *C*, travelling forward and keeping to the left to pass dancers *A* and *D*, execute two Pas de Basque RF, LF with *arms* in First Position (count '1 & 2, 3 & 4') or, alternatively, two Progressive Reel movements RF, LF with *arms* in Third Position (count '&1 & 2, &3 & 4') to finish facing inwards at points *1* and *4* respectively, then stand in First Position of the feet, *arms* and *head* for the remaining fourteen bars of Part 1.

Bars 9 to 11—A and D dance the Propelled Pivot Turn to the right, making approximately one and a half turns, finishing in a direct line with *C* and *B* (count '1 & 2 & 3 & 4 & 5 & 6').

Bar 12—Relinquishing the arm hold, execute two High Cuts springing LF, RF, and making approximately a quarter turn to the right (count '7 & 8 &').

Arms

Third Position.

Bars 13 to 16—A and D dance the Propelled Pivot Turn to the left, making approximately one and three-quarters turns (count '1 & 2 & 3 & 4 & 5 & 6 & 7'). Relinquishing the arm hold on the count of '7' continue the movement to finish with *A* at point *3* facing *C*, and *D* at point *2* facing B (count '& 8').

Part 2
(Starts *B*→   ←*D*   *A*→   ←*C*)

Bars 1 to 8—All dance a Basic Reel Step.

Bars 9 to 16—B with *D* and *A* with *C* dance the Propelled Pivot Turn to the right, then to the left, as described in Bars 9 to 16 of Part 1, finishing with *B* and *C* facing each other at points *2* and *3* respectively, and with *D* and *A* facing inwards at points *1* and *4* respectively.

Part 3
(Starts *D*→   *B*→   ←*C*   ←*A*)

Bars 1 to 8—B and C dance a Basic Reel Step.

Bars 9 to 16—B and C dance the Propelled Pivot Turn to the right, then to the left, as described in Part 1, *B* finishing at point *3* facing *A*, and *C* finishing at point *2* facing *D*. *A* and *D* stand for the above 16 bars in First Position of the feet, arms and head.

Part 4
(Starts *D*→   ←*C*   *B*→   ←*A*)

Bars 1 to 8—All dance a Basic Reel Step.

Bars 9 to 16—A with *B* and *C* with *D* dance the Propelled Pivot Turn to the right, then to the left, as described in Part 2, finishing with *D* and *A* facing each other at points *2* and *3* respectively, and *B* and *C* facing inwards at points *4* and *1* respectively.

Part 5
(Starts *C*→   *D*→   ←*A*   ←*B*)

Bars 1 to 16—*D* and *A* dance as described for *B* and *C* in Part 3, finishing with *D* at point *3*
facing *B* and with *A* at point *2* facing *C*.
B and *C* stand throughout in First Position of the feet, arms and head.

Part 6
(Starts *C*→   ←*A*   *D*→   ←*B*)

Bars 1 to 16—All dance as for Part 2 finishing with *C* and *B* facing each other at points *2* and *3*
respectively and with *A* and *D* facing inwards at points *1* and *4* respectively.

Part 7
(Starts *A*→   *C*→   ←*B*   ←*D*)

Bars 1 to 16—As for Part 3, but *B* and *C* finish in starting positions.

Part 8
(Starts *A*→   ←*B*   *C*→   ←*D*)

Bars 1 to 8—All execute the Last Basic Reel Step (High Cutting) and finish as at the start, i.e.
A facing *B*, *C* facing *D*.
Bars 9 to 16—*A* with *B* and *C* with *D* dance the Propelled Pivot Turn to the right then to the
left as before but finish *B*, *A*, *D*, *C*, facing the front at points *1*, *2*, *3*, *4*, respectively.

FINISH
All stand in First Position (flat) of the feet and bow.

Note 1.—When begun from First Position of the feet, a Basic Reel Step which is described as
beginning with Hop will instead begin with Disassemble and, for a Basic Reel Step described as
beginning with Assemble or the Balance movement, preparation is made on the last count of
the Bar preceding that on which the Basic Reel Step begins, by extending the right foot towards
Second Aerial Position Low or to the Fourth Intermediate Aerial Position.

Note 2.—On the last two beats of a Setting Step the dancers should make a one-eighth turn to
the left, preparatory to starting the Propelled Pivot Turn.

When the Reel of Tulloch is performed as a separate dance, the dancers begin as shown
in the diagram.

B→   ←*D*

1   *2*   *3*   *4*

A→   ←*C*

REEL OF TULLOCH

A slightly forward and inward from point *1*, facing *C*, who is slightly forward and inward from point *4*; *B* slightly back and inward from point *1*, facing *D*, who is slightly back and inward from point *4*.

Introduction

Bars 1 to 4—All stand as above, ready for the bow (count 1 to 8')

Bars 5 and 6—*A* and *D* make a quarter of a turn to the left while *B* and *C* make a quarter turn to the right to face partners in First Position (flat) and bow (count '1, 2, 3, 4').

Bars 7 and 8—All return to starting position and acknowledge the dancer opposite with a modified bow (count '5, 6, 7, 8').

All follow the dance description given but during Bars 1 and 2 of the First Basic Reel Step which begins Part 1, dancers *A* and *D* face and travel to points *2* and *3* respectively while, during Bar 1, dancers *B* and *C* step RF diagonally backwards on to the Set Line at points *1* and *4* respectively, close LF to RF in First Position flat (count '1, 2') and stand thus for the remaining fifteen bars of Part 1, with *arms* in First Position.

CHAPTER THREE

Rudiments of Music

Teachers and students should be conversant with the following musical terms and their definitions:

Staff

The five parallel lines and the four spaces between them upon, or in which the notes of the music are depicted.

Bar

The Staff is divided by perpendicular lines called Bar-lines, into short sections of equal value in the sense that each section takes the same period of time to play. The portion of music between any two consecutive Bar-lines is termed a Bar, which is itself divided into equal portions called Beats.

Beat

One of the regular pulsations of the music, or one of the equal sub-divisions of a Bar.

Time

The maintaining of a regular, or equal interval between Beats.

Tempo

The speed at which the music is played, denoted either by the number of bars to the minute, or by a number giving the metronome time.

Accent

The emphasis placed on any particular beat. There are three accents in music, namely Strong, Medium and Weak. The strong accent occurs only once in each bar, and always on the first beat of the bar.

Rhythm

The regular or periodical recurrence of accents.

Notation

The notes most generally used in music suitable for dancing are:

| Semibreve | Minim | Crotchet | Quaver | Semi-quaver |

The value of each of these notes is half the value of the preceding note, in the order given above, thus, taking the Semi-breve as a standard, a Minim is half, a Crotchet a quarter, a Quaver an eighth, and a Semi-quaver a sixteenth of its value.

RUDIMENTS OF MUSIC

Time Signature

The indication, at the beginning of the music, or any portion of the music, which denotes the number of beats in each bar, and their value as a fraction of a Semi-breve. When figures are used, the top figure gives the number of beats in the bar, and the bottom figure their fractional value (see Notation).

Repeats

(*a*) The letters D.C., placed below the Staff under a double bar-line, indicate to the musician to return, from that point, to the beginning of the music; the letters D.S., when similarly placed, instruct the musician to return to the point in the music denoted by the sign ·$. .
(*b*) When a double bar-line is followed by two or four dots in the spaces of the staff, and the next double bar-line is preceded by two or four dots similarly placed, then the portion of music between these double bars is repeated.

COUNTING OF HIGHLAND DANCING STEPS OR MOVEMENTS TO MUSIC

It is essential that both the teacher and the student should understand the method of counting steps and movements to music, using the standard rhythms explained below, all of which refer to Common Time, since Strathspey and Reel tunes used for Highland Dancing are usually written with that time signature.

Note.—In Common Time, which is denoted by the letter C on the staff, there are four crotchets in the bar, the accents being: Strong, Weak, Medium, Weak. Common Time is the same as $\frac{4}{4}$ time.

Single Beat Rhythm

Gives one sound in the space of time occupied by one beat. Thus there are four single beats in a bar of music (each represented by a crotchet) and counted:

1,   2,   3,   4

Half-Beat Rhythm

Gives two sounds of equal value in the space of time occupied by a single beat in the music. Thus there are eight half-beats in a bar (each represented by a quaver) and counted:

1 & 2 & 3 & 4 &

Imperfect Half-Beat Rhythm

It has been found expedient to adopt the combination of (*a*) a semi-quaver, followed by a dotted quaver, with the beat falling on the semi-quaver, or (*b*) a dotted quaver, followed by a semi-quaver, with the beat falling on the dotted quaver, as half-beats when counting steps or movements to music. Although neither of these combinations gives the sound of half-beats in a strict musical sense, since they are of unequal value, the semi-quaver being a quarter of a single beat, and the dotted quaver three-quarters of a single beat, the time-value of either of the combinations still equals the time-value of one complete single beat.

Method (a)

The beat falling on the semi-quaver is frequently found in music for Highland Dancing, the counting being denoted as follows:

1&   2&   3&   4&

Method (b)

The beat falling on the dotted quaver is only occasionally found in music for Highland Dancing, the counting being denoted as follows:

&1   &2   &3   &4

Triple Beat Rhythm

Gives three sounds of equal value in the space of time occupied by a single beat. Thus there are twelve triple beats in the bar (represented by twelve quavers grouped in threes, with that number depicted above each group) and counted:

1 and a 2 and a 3 and a 4 and a

Note.—In the dances described in this book, Triple Beat Rhythm is not used in the counting of steps or movements to music, but it is widely used in other branches of dancing, good examples being the Irish Jig and Sailors' Hornpipe, which dances are frequently included at games or competitions.

Quadruple (or Quarter) Beat Rhythm

Gives four sounds of equal value in the space of time occupied by a single beat. Thus there are sixteen quadruple (or quarter) beats in the bar (each represented by a semi-quaver) and counted:

1 and and a 2 and and a 3 and and a 4 and and a

Note.—When an 'and' is shown in brackets, this signifies that there is no action by the dancer on that quarter beat, nor should it be sounded when counting.

NOTES

1   When denoting Triple Beat Rhythm or Quadruple Beat Rhythm, the writer deems it advisable to use the word 'and' fully written so that those rhythms may be quickly distinguished from Half-beat Rhythm and Imperfect Half-beat Rhythm, in both of which the ampersand '&' is invariably used.

RUDIMENTS OF MUSIC

2   It is customary to group two consecutive bars of music together for the purpose of counting a step or movement, in which case the counting for those two bars—in single beats—would be 1, 2, 3, 4, 5, 6, 7, 8.

3   In any movement, when two actions are executed almost simultaneously (for example a 'Spring Point'), these actions are counted as if they were executed simultaneously, i.e. to one count.

4   When executing any movement of elevation, the dancer should land on the count, except on the few occasions where otherwise stated.

5   When the working foot has to be placed in or raised to any specified position while executing a movement of elevation, that foot arrives at the specified position simultaneously with the dancer landing on the supporting foot unless otherwise stated.

6   Although Reel tunes are usually written in Common Time, they are played at a tempo so much faster than Strathspey tunes that it is found expedient to count steps or movements executed to Reel tunes as if the music were written in $\frac{2}{4}$ Time, that is to say, counting two in the bar so that crotchets count as half-beats and minims as single beats. Consequently, for the same movements or steps, we get the same counting, no matter whether that movement or step is executed to Strathspey Tempo or Reel Tempo. For example, the counting for a Pas de Basque is 1 & 2, 3 & 4 whether that movement is danced to Strathspey Tempo or to Reel Tempo, yet that Pas de Basque occupies only half a bar when danced to Strathspey Tempo and a complete bar when danced to Reel Tempo.

CHAPTER FOUR

Competitions

The rules and conditions recommended for competitions set forth in this chapter are those which have been adopted by the Scottish Official Board of Highland Dancing.

A Professional competition is one in which only professional dancers may compete; an Amateur competition is one in which only amateur dancers may compete; a Mixed competition is one in which both professional and amateur dancers may compete. If the title of a competition does not indicate that it is confined either to professional or amateur dancers, it shall be regarded as a Mixed competition.

A. Rules and Conditions

1 Championships

(*a*) A Championship recognised by the Board must include at least three of the following dances and if only three dances are used in a Championship, they must be the first three in the order mentioned:

Highland Fling

Sword Dance (Gillie Chalium)

Seann Triubhas

Strathspey or Reel of Tulloch; or Strathspey and Highland Reel or Reel of Tulloch; or
    Strathspey and Highland Reel and Reel of Tulloch.

(*b*) No competition in Highland Dancing may be entitled 'Championship' without the sanction of the Board.

(*c*) Championships must be held under the Scottish Official Board of Highland Dancing rules and must be advertised as 'Recognised by the S.O.B.H.D.'

2 Titles of Championships

Titles of Championships are limited to the following five classes:

WORLD—Traditionally held at the Cowal Games.

NATIONAL—Covering a whole country or more.

AREA—Covering a large geographical area of a country such as North, South, East, West or Midlands; in which case the boundary of such area must coincide with county boundaries. The boundary of a proposed Area Championship must be clearly defined by the organisers and must receive the approval of the Board.

COUNTY—Covering one geographical county. The Board may sanction two adjacent counties holding one combined Championship, e.g. Sutherland and Caithness.

ADDITIONAL TITLES—Selected according to aptitude, e.g. 'Land o' Burns'.

3 Open and Closed Championships

(*a*) An Open Championship is one in which competitors resident outwith the area named in its title may compete. A Closed Championship is one in which the competitor must qualify by birth or by having been resident for twelve months immediately prior to the event in the county, area or country covered by the Championship. Unless otherwise laid down by the organisers, there is no maximum or minimum age limit for competitors in an Open or a Closed Championship.

(*b*) When a person is qualified to compete in two County Championships—one by birth and one by residence—such person may not compete during any one calendar year in both Championships but must make his or her choice. The choice shall also determine which Closed Area Championship such person is entitled to enter.

(*c*) National and Area Championships may be either open or closed at the discretion of the organisers. If both are sanctioned by the Board they must be organised as separate events.

(*d*) County Championships may be open or closed at the discretion of the Board, but only one of such types will be sanctioned during any one calendar year for any particular county.

4 Recognition of Championships

(*a*) Application to the Board for recognition of a competition as a Championship must be made in writing to reach the Board not less than three calendar months prior to the date set for that competition and must designate the FULL NAME and DESCRIPTION of the organising party and give the DATE, VENUE, CLASSIFICATION and TYPE (Open or Closed) of the proposed Championship.

(*b*) Should the organising party desire to hold *more than one championship at the same venue* on the same date, the details of each championship applied for may be set forth on the one application.

(*c*) Every application must be accompanied by a registration fee of One Guinea (£1 1s.) in respect of each championship applied for (see also Rule 12), but should the Board refuse the recognition of a championship applied for, the registration fee shall be returned.

(*d*) A championship sanctioned by the Board may be held once only in any one calendar year.

(*e*) When applying for the RENEWAL OF RECOGNITION of a championship, the organising party shall follow the same procedure as laid down in paragraphs (*a*), (*b*), and (*c*) above.

5 Unrecognised 'Championships'

A competitor who has taken part in any so-called championship not recognised by the Board, or any person who has acted as judge at such an event, shall be ineligible to compete or adjudicate respectively in any recognised championship until given permission to do so by the Board. Such permission may be withheld for so long as the Board may decide.

6 Competitions other than Championships

If a competition other than a championship is to be conducted according to the rules recommended by the S.O.B.H.D. the promoter shall be entitled to advertise to that effect.

7 Entry Forms

Entry forms in respect of a competition approved by the Board or conducted under Board rules should be so worded that on signing same the competitor (or parent or guardian on behalf of a competitor under 18 years of age) thereby agrees to accept and to act in accordance with the said rules as far as they may affect that competition.

8 Judging

(*a*) The judges for a championship must be selected from the Panel of Judges appointed by the Board. Failure to carry out this condition, unless a satisfactory explanation be given, shall nullify the event and jeopardise the renewal of recognition.

(*b*) Throughout the course of any championship, unless otherwise sanctioned by the Board, there must be at least three judges who shall mark independently. If for any unforeseen reason an appointed judge is unable to officiate, and if it is found impossible to fill his or her place with an eligible judge, the remaining judges shall act, and the circumstances shall be announced to the competitors prior to the competition, and an explanation sent to the Board.

(*c*) A professional who acts as a judge at a professional championship is thereafter debarred from competing in a professional championship. (See also *addendum*, p. 82.)

9 Definition and Rights of an Amateur

(i) An Amateur is one who:

(*a*) Has never been employed or engaged or accepted remuneration, either in money or kind, as a dancer; has never been engaged in the teaching of dancing, or an assistant to a teacher of dancing; or has not acted as organiser or judge of a competition for personal profit.

(*b*) Has never taken part in a competition for which a money prize is offered (see para. (ii) (*a*)), or in connection with which expenses of any kind are paid to competitors, excepting such expenses as are sanctioned by the Board and described in para. (ii) (*b*).

(*c*) Has never sold or converted into money a prize won for dancing.

(*d*) Has never declared himself or herself to be a professional by advertisment or otherwise. Participation in a competition or match limited to professionals shall be taken as such a declaration. The passing of the entrance examination to any Branch of an Examining Body, e.g. a dance teachers' association, or the taking of any examination confined to dance professionals, shall be regarded as a definite act of professionalism. The fact that a person is training as a student with a view to taking a professional examination, shall not jeopardise his or her amateur status.

(ii) Amateurs have the following rights:

(*a*) They are permitted to participate in mixed and general competitions for which money prizes are given to professionals provided an amateur receives no money as a prize and provided it is declared in the conditions of the competition that, in the event of an amateur winning a prize, such prize will not include any money.

(*b*) In the event of an amateur accepting an invitation to compete in a competition to be held in a town other than that in which he or she resides, then such amateur shall be allowed to accept the following expenses from the organiser of that competition:

COMPETITIONS

    (1) Bare travelling expenses from the town in which the amateur resides, to and from the town in which the competition is being held.

    (2) Bare hotel expenses incurred in the town in which the competition is being held, limited to the day or days of the competition and to one day before and one day after.

Note.—The above expenses must be in reimbursement of actual expenses personally incurred by the amateur in respect of himself or herself only.

10   Classification of Competitors

The following classifications apply to all competitors who are seven years of age or over and are thus outwith the Baby age-group of six years and under in which there are no classifications.

Beginner—A competitor who is seven years of age or over is classified as a Beginner until gaining a prize in three separate Beginners' competitions, after which that dancer is classified as a Novice and is ineligible to enter for any further Beginners' competitions.

Novice—This status may be held until the competitor gains a prize in three separate Novice competitions, after which that competitor is classified as an Intermediate and is ineligible to enter for any competitions confined to Beginners or Novices.

Intermediate—This status may be held until the competitor gains a prize in three separate Intermediate competitions, after which that competitor is eligible to enter for Open competitions only.

Proviso—Should a competitor in the Baby (under seven years) age-group take part in a competition for a higher age-group then, when so doing, that competitor shall compete under the above rules as if he or she actually belonged to the higher age-group, and any prize thus gained shall be taken into account when taking part in any further competitions for a higher age-group.

Furthermore, if as a result of dancing in competitions for a higher age-group, that competitor loses Beginner status therein, then whatever classification is ultimately attained (Novice, Intermediate or Open as the case may be) shall apply to him or her on reaching the age of seven years.

11   Sequence of Steps

In each dance at a Championship, competitors shall dance the same steps in the sequence laid down by the Board for the calendar year in which the Championship is taking place. This not only materially assists the judges in arriving at a decision, but looks better from the spectators' point of view.

The steps in each dance are named and numbered in Chapter Two of this book and the organising party should, in good time prior to the event, give notice of these steps that are to be performed and the sequence required. The Board shall include one or two different steps each year so that competitors will ultimately become conversant with all the steps recognised by the Board, none of which will be liable to fall into disuse. It should be borne in mind that (the last step in the Seann Triubhas excepted) the recognised first and last steps in each dance, as described in Chapter Two, must be retained as such.

12   Certificates

The winner of a recognised Championship shall be entitled to a certificate issued by the Board and signed by the Chairman of the Board. Should the organiser so desire, the Board shall supply certificates for the second, third and fourth prize winners at a cost to the organiser of 1s. in respect of each extra certificate ordered. Should the organiser of a recognised Championship held outwith the United Kingdom desire that the certificates for same be sent by air-mail, then an additional 5s. must be included along with the registration fee for each Championship concerned.

The organising party is responsible for:

(a) Providing the Board, within seven days of the event, with full particulars with which to complete the certificates.

(b) Forwarding the completed certificates to the respective winners as soon as possible after receiving them from the Board.

13   Judge's Decision

Subject to Rule 14 (b) below, the decision of a judge is final and no discussion or correspondence can be entered into between a judge and a competitor or the parent or guardian of a competitor regarding any decision made by that judge.

14   Objections

(a) An objection to a person's eligibility to compete in any particular competition must be made in writing and shall not be considered unless the complainant gives his or her full name and address accompanied by a deposit of One Guinea (£1 1s.) which shall be returned should the objection be sustained. Such objection must be lodged with the organiser of the event concerned if possible before the event and certainly not later than seven days after the date of the event. Unless admitted by the person complained about, the organiser shall refer the matter to the Board, but if there is not time for the Board to reach a decision before the event takes place, then the person complained about shall be permitted to dance in the competition on the understanding that any awards he or she may win therein shall be withheld until the decision of the Board be known. Should the objection be sustained, those awards shall be passed down to the competitor next in order of merit and the other awards suitably adjusted.

(b) Any complaint made by an individual against the organisation or adjudication of an event shall be made in writing giving the complainant's full name and address, and shall be lodged with the organiser if possible on the day of the event and certainly not later than forty-eight hours after the event. Such complaint must be accompanied by a deposit of One Guinea (£1 1s.) which shall be returned should the complaint be upheld. If within seven days of lodging such complaint, the complainant has received no satisfaction from the organiser, then the complainant may refer the matter to the Hon. Secretary of the Board.

(c) Any complaint made by an association against the organisation or adjudication of an event shall be sent direct in writing to the Hon. Secretary of the Board as soon as possible and not later than forty-eight hours after the first meeting held by that association following the event concerned. When sending such complaint to the Board, a copy of same shall be sent by the Association to the organiser or judge against whom the complaint is directed.

15 Alteration to Rules

No alteration to the foregoing Rules and Conditions shall come into force until the first day of January after such alteration has received the assent of two-thirds of those present at a meeting of the Board and has previously been set out in the Agenda for that meeting.

16 General

Should any point arise not covered in the foregoing Rules and Conditions, it shall be referred to the Board whose decision shall be final.

B. Recommendations

1 Accommodation and Marshalling of Competitors

(*a*) Suitable changing and toilet accommodation should be provided for competitors.

(*b*) An official should be appointed for the purpose of marshalling competitors.

2 Size of Platform

The minimum dimensions of the dancing platform should be as follows:

Breadth	24 feet
Depth	18 feet
Height	$2\frac{1}{2}$ feet

3 Equipment

Highland broadswords should invariably be used for the Sword Dance (Gillie Chalium) and the organising party should endeavour to provide a sufficient number of such, i.e. for three dancers per platform.

No medals may be worn by competitors prior to the conclusion of the judging of any competition or championship.

4 Maximum Number of Dancers on Platform

Highland Fling	Heats—4 Finals—4 (If 5 dancers are recalled for a final, all may dance together provided there is ample platform space.)
Sword Dance	Heats—3 Finals—3 (recommended 2 only)
Seann Triubhas	Heats—3 Finals—3 (recommended 2 only)
Strathspey and/or Reel	Heats and Finals—one set only (4 dancers)

5 Sequence of Steps

The Board strongly recommends that Rule 11 of *A* should apply also to competitions other than championships.

6   Position of Judges

In order to secure independent decisions, judges should be so placed that, whilst having an uninterrupted view of the competitors, they are unable to communicate with each other by any means whilst judging is in progress.

During a competition, from the time the first heat begins until the final has been danced, no person should be allowed to contact the judges except the scrutineer or the steward authorised to collect the judges' marking sheets on behalf of the scrutineer.

7   Judges' Marking

(*a*) In each dance there shall be a maximum of 100 marks which may be allocated under the following three headings:

Timing	Maximum marks—10
Technique	Maximum marks—80
General Deportment	Maximum marks—10

Organisers should supply judges with judging cards (see specimen on page 79) in which the second, third and fourth columns may be used by the judges to take note of any faults under the relevant heading which influence their marking; but it is not obligatory for judges to enter a specific mark in those columns.

Where a heat of any competition is concerned, judges must enter the aggregate mark for each competitor in column five.

In a final, judges may use an aggregate mark as a guide to deciding on the placings (1st, 2nd, 3rd and so on up to the number taking part). The placing must be entered in column six.

(*b*) If a judge alters a marking, such alteration must be clearly initialled. Marking sheets should be handed to the steward before judges leave their seats and they cannot be altered thereafter unless to correct any error of detail discovered by the scrutineer.

(*c*) If in the opinion of a judge, the standard of dancing shown by a competitor is so much below average that such competitor stands no chance of being placed, the judge need not award marks to that competitor.

(*d*) If, during the course of a re-dance with two competitors who have tied for a specific placing in a Sword Dance final, one of those competitors displaces the swords, then the resultant disqualification shall apply only to the re-dance and not to the competition proper, in which that competitor shall be given the next lowest placing to that gained by the winner of the re-dance.

(*e*) Where more experienced competitors are concerned, the Board recommends the following standard for judges' markings:

A good performance	70–75 marks
A very good performance	76–80 marks
A distinguished performance	81–85 marks
An outstanding performance	86 marks or over

Note.—Few competitors will attain 95 marks or over.

COMPETITIONS

JUDGE'S CARD

Title of Championship: Place.................................

....   Date.................................

Class............... Section............... Dance............... Judge........................

Competitors' No.	Timing 10	Technique 80	General Deportment 10	Total	Placing for final

SCRUTINEERING SHEET

Title of Championship: Place...

....   Date.............. ....

Class............... Section...............   Dance...

Competitors No.	Aggregate Mark or Placing JUDGE			Total	Result
	A	B	C		

8 Scrutineering

A specimen scrutineer's sheet is shown on page 79.

(*a*) When the ultimate placings in a competition are dependent on the results of heat finals then, for placings in those finals, points shall be awarded as under:

1st Place	.	.	.	8 points
2nd Place	.	.	.	5 points
3rd Place	.	.	.	3 points
4th Place	.	.	.	1 point

In the event of a tie between two competitors for any specific placing, both competitors will receive the total points awarded for the relevant placing and the next lowest placing is omitted.

(*b*) When a heat embraces fewer than 50 competitors, there will be no necessity for a final therein, provided the scrutineer is able to select the 1st, 2nd, 3rd and 4th placings from the judges' markings. However, if the scrutineer is unable to do so or, if the heat embraces 50 or more competitors, the scrutineer shall select a short leet to dance in a heat final if such is required, or to pass on to take part in a grand final.

(*c*) If, when the ultimate placings for a competition are being resolved from the results of heat finals, it is found that two competitors have the same number of points for 1st place then, if one competitor gained more 1st placings in heat finals than the other, the competitor with the majority of such placings shall take 1st place in the competition proper and the other competitor will take 2nd place. Should that procedure still result in a tie, the aggregate marks awarded in the various heats may be taken into consideration and the competitor with the highest aggregate total shall be the winner.

Should there be a tie for any other specific placing, the procedure in connection with that placing shall be similar to that outlined above for 1st place.

(*d*) Should the competition be carried out on different lines i.e. without heat finals but with a short leet being selected from each heat to dance in a grand final embracing the dances concerned, then in the final for each dance points shall be awarded as laid down in para. (*a*) above and, in the event of a tie, the same procedure shall be followed as outlined in para. (*c*) above with each dance being regarded as a heat final.

(*e*) Should any point arise not covered in the above recommendations, the matter shall be left for the judges to decide and their decision shall be final but before arriving at a decision, the judges may consult the organiser if they deem it advisable to do so.

C. *Aids to Judges*

The technique compiled by the Board is the result of embodying what is considered to be the best of many styles, yet it allows an appreciable variation in the method of presentation and considerable scope for individual interpretation. Therefore, provided a competitor conforms to that technique, judges must not allow personal stylistic preference to bias their judgment.

COMPETITIONS

Timing—The keeping of good time to the music in the performance of arm movements and, in particular, those of the feet.

Technique—Correct execution incorporating footwork in conjunction with head, arm and hand movement.

Footwork demands the correct placing of the feet during the performance. The ability to apply the recognised ground and aerial foot positions is the foundation upon which all good dancing is built, so it is essential that they be closely adhered to throughout. No matter how superficially showy a movement may appear it is never really attractive if performed 'out of position'. Judges should bear in mind that the supporting foot should be as closely watched as the working foot.

General Deportment—This covers 'interpretation' (the ability of the dancer to express the spirit and motif of the dance), 'balance', 'general appearance' and 'comportment', thus embracing carriage of the head, arms, body and hands; and in particular including:

(i) Pleasure in the dance.

(ii) Supple movement with lack of strain.

(iii) Upright carriage.

(iv) Freedom from elaborate 'showiness'.

(v) Apparent 'unhurriedness' in dancing.

(vi) Buoyancy without exaggerated elevation.

Adherence to the following points would help achieve uniformity in judging:

(*a*) Prior to a competition, judges should get together and agree on a standard for each age group, e.g. a top mark of 75 for competitors 7 years and under; a top mark of 85 for competitors 12 years and under; all others a top mark of 100.

(*b*) Judges should make sure the swords are properly placed and not too near the edge of the platform.

(*c*) If, in order to make up the requisite number for a set in a Strathspey, Highland Reel or Reel of Tulloch, it is necessary for a competitor to dance twice (or oftener) in the same heat, semi-final or final, such competitor shall be judged on his or her first appearance before the judges in that heat, semi-final or final.

(*d*) Competitors may be requested to stand in their places at the end of each dance until given permission by the judges to leave the platform. This particularly applies in Strathspeys and/or Reels. When this procedure is in operation, judges should fill in their markings as quickly as possible to avoid holding up the competition.

(*e*) Should a competitor, on making a mistake in a Strathspey or Reel, thereby upset the rest of the set, the judges shall stop the dance forthwith and order a re-dance to take place later on with a substitute for the defaulting competitor who shall be disqualified in that dance.

(*f*) Should a mistake on the part of the piper have an adverse effect on the performance of competitors, the judges may order a re-dance or otherwise deal with the matter at their discretion.

(*g*) Provided due prominence is given to the fact in the programme or in a brochure issued by the organiser, then during the course of a competition the comportment of competitors may come under the jurisdiction of the judges, not only whilst dancing, but also when entering or leaving the platform and whilst waiting on the dance to start. Any unseemly behaviour on the part of a competitor or any misdemeanour likely to upset the decorum of the proceedings may be penalised by the judges and could lead to disqualification but a full report of any such misconduct on the part of a competitor must be submitted by the judges to the organiser.

Penalties

The following penalties are recommended by the Board.

(*a*) A deduction of 5 marks should be made for:

Missing the start.

Temporarily dancing off time.

Placing the swords wrongly.

Touching the swords during the dance.

Shoe coming off.

Hose coming down.

Hat, sporran or any part of equipment falling off.

(*b*) Disqualification should result from:

Dancing the wrong step during a Championship.

Dancing steps in the wrong sequence during a Championship.

Dancing a non-Board step.

Falling or tripping.

Stopping momentarily during the progress of a dance.

Dancing off time consistently.

Displacing one's own swords.

Displacing the swords of another competitor.

Note.—If a competitor's swords are displaced by another dancer, that competitor shall be allowed to re-dance.

Alterations to Recommendations

No alteration to the contents of *B* or *C* above shall come into force until the first day of January after such alteration has been agreed upon at a meeting of the Board and has previously been set out on the agenda of that meeting.

Addendum to Rule 8, p. 74.

(*d*) Prior to retiring from competative dancing, a member of the Board's Judges' Panel can officiate only at a competition or championship in which all the competitors are under 16 years of age.

CHAPTER FIVE

Dress for Highland Dancers

(As recommended by the Board)

The recognised forms of dress for male Highland dancers have not altered appreciably in use and practice during the last century, and little requires to be said about them. However, a general description will not go amiss.

Males

TYPE 1

Jacket—May be of velvet or cloth in any colour and any recognised style of doublet or coatee. Garments are generally, but not always, worn with a dirk belt with which a dirk may or may not be used at the discretion of the wearer.

Kilt—Any clan or family tartan.

Sporran—Evening pattern, usually sealskin with plated metal top. Hair full dress sporran is *not* correct for competitive dancers.

Stockings—Tartan, to match kilt.

Garter flashes—Red or green.

Head dress—Balmoral or glengarry bonnet, with appropriate crest. The clan badge may be worn behind the crest. Feathers should not be worn.

Skean dhu—Worn if desired.

Footwear—Black Highland dancing pumps.

Plaid—Belted plaid may be worn at the discretion of the dancer.

Jabot—In lace, or a black bow tie are optional.

Ruffles—Optional if jabot is worn and must be attached to the sleeve of the shirt or coat.

TYPE 2

Jacket and waistcoat—Day wear style, in Lovat or other type of tweed.

Kilt—Any clan or family tartan.

Sporran—Leather, any pattern.

Stockings—Plain to tone with jacket, or marl leg with tartan top.

Skean dhu—Worn if desired.

Footwear—Black Highland dancing pumps.

TYPE 3

The outfit as in Type 2 may be worn without the jacket and waistcoat, and with a white shirt and tartan or other tie.

DRESS FOR HIGHLAND DANCING

Females

The dress for female Highland dancers may consist only of skirt and white blouse, but a jacket or a waistcoat may be worn over the blouse. The legs may be bare or hose may be worn.

Skirt—Kilt reaching to the centre of the knee.

Note.—A plain kilt-pin should be used to fasten the kilt.

White blouse—Full or half-length sleeves as desired, with a lace-ornamented front and a lace stand at the back of the neck. The lace stand is an upright stiffened lace half-collar, approximately $1\frac{1}{4}$ in. in depth, attached to the blouse.

Jacket—Black or coloured velvet with no outside pockets, close fitting at the waist and hips, and fastened only at the waist, the basque having two points in front and wide scallops. The jacket is trimmed round the edges with a single row of $\frac{1}{2}$ in. silver braid. The facings have a single row of not more than five ornamental buttons on each side. The full length sleeves may have a single row of not more than five silver buttons at the vent. If desired, ruffles (not exceeding 1 in. in depth) may be worn at the wrist, but they must be fastened to the sleeve.

Waistcoat—Similar to the jacket as described above, but without sleeves, there being no trimming round the armholes.

Head dress—A Balmoral-type bonnet, made of soft material to match the jacket, may be worn.

Hose—If worn, may be (*a*) full tartan; (*b*) marl leg with a tartan top; or (*c*) long hose.

Footwear—Black Highland dancing pumps.

Underwear—Dark or tartan trews should be worn.

Note.—The front edges of the jacket are boned from the waist up and elastic loops are fitted inside to fasten to the top of the kilt in order to prevent the jacket from rising when the arms are raised.

The following items should *not* be worn:

Skean dhu	Plaid	Bows
Sporran	Flashes	Other ornaments of
Belt	Bonnet	any description